DRUG TRANSIT AND DISTRIBUTION, INTERCEPTION AND CONTROL

PRESCRIPTION DRUGS AND THE DEA

INTERACTIONS AND ISSUES WITH CONTROLLED SUBSTANCES REGISTRANTS

DRUG TRANSIT AND DISTRIBUTION, INTERCEPTION AND CONTROL

Additional books in this series can be found on Nova's website under the Series tab.

Additional e-books in this series can be found on Nova's website under the e-book tab.

DRUG TRANSIT AND DISTRIBUTION, INTERCEPTION AND CONTROL

PRESCRIPTION DRUGS AND THE DEA

INTERACTIONS AND ISSUES WITH CONTROLLED SUBSTANCES REGISTRANTS

KARA MORRIS
EDITOR

nova publishers
New York

Library of Congress Cataloging-in-Publication Data

ISBN: 978-1-63484-606-6

Published by Nova Science Publishers, Inc. † New York

CONTENTS

PREFACE

The Drug Enforcement Administration (DEA) administers and enforces the Controlled Substances Act (CSA) as it pertains to ensuring the availability of controlled substances, including certain prescription drugs, for legitimate use while limiting their availability for abuse and diversion. The CSA requires those handling controlled substances to register with DEA. This book examines to what extent registrants interact with DEA about their CSA responsibilities, and registrants' perspectives on those interactions; how state agencies and national associations interact with DEA, and their perspectives on those interactions; and stakeholders' perspectives on how DEA enforcement actions have affected prescription drug abuse and diversion and access to those drugs for legitimate needs. The book also highlights certain non-criminal regulatory requirements.

In: Prescription Drugs and the DEA
Editor: Kara Morris
ISBN: 978-1-63484-606-6

Chapter 1

PRESCRIPTION DRUGS: MORE DEA INFORMATION ABOUT REGISTRANTS' CONTROLLED SUBSTANCES ROLES COULD IMPROVE THEIR UNDERSTANDING AND HELP ENSURE ACCESS*

United States Government Accountability Office

WHY GAO DID THIS STUDY

The Drug Enforcement Agency (DEA) administers and enforces the Controlled Substances Act (CSA) as it pertains to ensuring the availability of controlled substances, including certain prescription drugs, for legitimate use while limiting their availability for abuse and diversion. The CSA requires those handling controlled substances to register with DEA.

GAO was asked to review registrants' and others' interactions with DEA. This report examines (1) to what extent registrants interact with DEA about their CSA responsibilities, and registrants' perspectives on those interactions, (2) how state agencies and national associations interact with DEA, and their perspectives on those interactions, and (3) stakeholders' perspectives on how DEA enforcement actions have affected prescription drug abuse and diversion

* This is an edited, reformatted and augmented version of the United States Government Accountability Office publication, GAO-15-471, dated June 2015.

and access to those drugs for legitimate needs. GAO administered nationally representative web-based surveys to DEA-registered distributors, individual pharmacies, chain pharmacy corporate offices, and practitioners. GAO also interviewed officials from DEA, 26 national associations and other nonprofits, and 16 government agencies in four states representing varying geographic regions and overdose death rates.

WHAT GAO RECOMMENDS

GAO recommends that DEA take three actions to improve communication with and guidance for registrants about their CSA roles and responsibilities. DEA described actions that it planned to take to implement GAO's recommendations; however, GAO identified additional actions DEA should take to fully implement the recommendations.

WHAT GAO FOUND

GAO's four nationally representative surveys of Drug Enforcement Administration (DEA) registrants showed that these registrants vary in the extent of their interaction with DEA related to their roles and responsibilities for preventing prescription drug abuse and diversion under the Controlled Substances Act (CSA). Specifically, GAO found that distributors and chain pharmacy corporate offices interacted with DEA more often than individual pharmacies or health care practitioners. The surveys also showed that many registrants are not aware of various DEA resources. For example, GAO estimates that 70 percent of practitioners are not aware of DEA's Practitioner's Manual. Of those registrants that have interacted with DEA, most were generally satisfied with those interactions. For example, 92 percent of distributors that communicated with DEA field office staff found them "very" or "moderately" helpful. However, some distributors, individual pharmacies, and chain pharmacy corporate offices want improved guidance from, and additional communication with, DEA about their CSA roles and responsibilities. For example, 36 of 55 distributors commented that more communication or information from, or interactions with, DEA would be helpful. DEA officials indicated that they do not believe there is a need for more registrant guidance or communication. Federal internal control standards call for adequate communication with stakeholders. Without more registrant awareness of DEA resources and adequate guidance and communication from DEA, registrants may not fully understand or meet their CSA roles and responsibilities.

Officials GAO interviewed from 14 of 16 state government agencies and 24 of 26 national associations said that they interact with DEA through various methods. Thirteen of 14 state agencies and 10 of 17 national associations that commented about their satisfaction with DEA interactions said that they were generally satisfied; however, some associations wanted improved DEA communication. Because the additional communication that four associations want relates to their members' CSA roles and responsibilities, improved DEA communication with and guidance for registrants may address some of the associations' concerns.

Among those offering a perspective, between 31 and 38 percent of registrants GAO surveyed and 13 of 17 state agencies and national associations GAO interviewed believe that DEA enforcement actions have helped decrease prescription drug abuse and diversion. GAO's survey results also showed that over half of DEA registrants have changed certain business practices as a result of DEA enforcement actions or the business climate these actions may have created. For example, GAO estimates that over half of distributors placed stricter limits on the quantities of controlled substances that their customers (e.g., pharmacies) could order, and that most of these distributors (84 percent) were influenced to a "great" or "moderate extent" by DEA's enforcement actions. Many individual pharmacies (52 of 84) and chain pharmacy corporate offices (18 of 29) reported that these stricter limits have limited, to a "great" or "moderate extent," their ability to supply drugs to those with legitimate needs. While DEA officials said they generally did not believe that enforcement actions have negatively affected access, better communication and guidance from DEA could help registrants make business decisions that balance ensuring access for patients with legitimate needs with controlling abuse and diversion.

ABBREVIATIONS

ARCOS	Automated Reports and Consolidated Orders System
CDC	Centers for Disease Control and Prevention
CMS	Centers for Medicare & Medicaid Services
CSA	Controlled Substances Act

DEA	Drug Enforcement Administration
PDAC	Pharmacy Diversion Awareness Conference

***

June 25, 2015

Congressional Requesters

The Centers for Disease Control and Prevention (CDC) has declared that the United States is in the midst of an epidemic of prescription drug overdose deaths. In 2013, more than 22,000 Americans died from drug overdoses attributable to prescription drugs, and most of those deaths— more than 16,000—were attributable to prescription opioid pain relievers. While these prescription drugs have legitimate purposes and are safe when taken as directed, they also can be misused, and pose a potential for abuse and addiction as well as being diverted for illicit uses.[1] In 2012, an estimated 6.8 million Americans reported being current nonmedical users of prescription drugs, according to the National Survey on Drug Use and Health. About 70 percent of these people reportHed that they got the drug from a friend or family member, while about 22 percent got the drug from a doctor.[2] Abuse of prescription drugs results in significant social, public health, and economic consequences for the United States. For example, economic costs include workplace costs (e.g., lost productivity), health care costs (e.g., abuse treatment), and criminal justice costs. One study estimated that opioid pain reliever abuse costs health insurers alone up to $72.5 billion per year.[3]

Multiple federal agencies have responsibility for addressing the misuse, abuse, and diversion of prescription drugs through prevention, treatment, and enforcement activities. In particular, the Department of Justice's Drug Enforcement Administration (DEA) has a key role as it enforces the Controlled Substances Act (CSA). The CSA was enacted in 1970 to regulate and facilitate the use of controlled substances, including certain prescription drugs such as opioid pain relievers, for legitimate medical, scientific, research, and industrial purposes while preventing them from being diverted for illegal uses.[4] DEA's Office of Diversion Control is responsible for administering and enforcing the provisions of the CSA as they pertain to ensuring the availability of controlled substances for legitimate uses while limiting their availability for abuse and diversion. Various CSA provisions require persons who handle controlled substances to register with the DEA, including businesses that import, export, manufacture, or distribute controlled substances; health care practitioners, such as physicians, licensed to dispense, administer, or prescribe them; and pharmacies authorized to fill prescriptions.[5] These DEA registrants have certain responsibilities under the CSA and its implementing regulations for preventing abuse and diversion of controlled substances. For example, practitioner registrants must ensure that prescriptions for controlled substances are issued for legitimate medical purposes. To monitor registrants' compliance with the CSA, DEA can conduct investigations into instances of potential diversion, and can initiate a variety of enforcement actions for violations of the CSA and its implementing regulations. DEA also conducts educational activities and provides guidance to its registrants regarding their roles and responsibilities under the CSA.

Because the problem of prescription drug abuse is complex and multi-faceted, a federal report has noted that an effective response to the problem requires a multi-pronged approach that can only be achieved through a coordinated effort among public health, clinical medicine, public safety, and other stakeholders.[6] Accordingly, in addition to its work with registrants, DEA interacts with other governmental and nongovernmental stakeholders, such as state public health and law enforcement agencies, and national associations representing various interests, on efforts related to reducing prescription drug abuse and diversion. However, questions have been raised about how and the extent to which DEA interacts with its registrants and other nonfederal stakeholders on issues related to reducing prescription drug abuse and diversion, as well as whether DEA's enforcement actions have struck the right balance between reducing diversion and ensuring access for legitimate medical needs.

You asked us to review registrants' interactions with DEA related to their responsibilities under the CSA, DEA's coordination of efforts with nonfederal stakeholders to reduce prescription drug abuse and diversion, and the effect of enforcement actions on abuse and diversion and access to prescription drugs. This report examines (1) how and to what extent selected registrants interact with DEA related to their responsibilities for preventing prescription drug abuse and diversion under the CSA, and registrants' perspectives on those interactions, (2) how selected state agencies and national associations interact with DEA related to reducing prescription drug abuse and diversion, and their perspectives on those interactions, and (3) stakeholders' perspectives about how DEA enforcement actions have affected abuse and diversion of prescription drugs and access to those drugs for legitimate medical needs. For the purposes of this report, the stakeholders whose perspectives we obtained include DEA registrants (distributors, pharmacies, and practitioners),[7] state government officials in four states, and officials from 26 national associations and other nonprofits representing various interests.[8]

To address our first and third objectives, we administered four web-based nationally representative surveys to the following three types of DEA registrants: distributors, pharmacies, and practitioners. Using DEA's CSA registrant database as of January 2014 to create listings of these populations, we split the pharmacy population into two—"individual" pharmacies and "chain pharmacy corporate offices." We defined the individual pharmacies as being individually registered pharmacy locations that were either independently owned or part of a corporation with less than 50 registered pharmacy locations, and we defined the chain pharmacy corporate offices as having 50 or more registered pharmacy locations. We surveyed generalizable random samples of 200 distributors, 304 individual pharmacies, and 400 practitioners.[9] The 304 individual pharmacies were asked to respond to the survey on behalf of their single pharmacy location that was selected in our sample, regardless of its ownership status. We also surveyed all of the corporate offices of the 38 chain pharmacies we identified, using DEA's CSA database, as having 50 or more registered pharmacy locations.[10] These 38 chain pharmacy corporate offices were asked to respond to the survey on behalf of all of their registered pharmacy locations. We conducted our surveys between July 2014 and October 2014. The response rates for each registrant sample were as follows: 86 percent of distributors, 63 percent of individual pharmacies, and 55 percent of practitioners.[11] Among the chain pharmacy corporate offices we surveyed, 84 percent (32 of 38) responded. We selected these categories of registrants because they are the primary DEA registrants in the prescription drug supply chain and are more likely to be the focus of DEA enforcement actions than other categories of registrants such as researchers or drug importers.[12] We surveyed registrants about how they have interacted with DEA since 2012, and their perspectives about those interactions. We also surveyed registrants about their perspectives on how DEA enforcement actions, or the possibility of actions against registrants, have affected their business practices, or the business climate in which they operate, as well as their perspectives on whether enforcement actions have had an effect on reducing abuse and diversion and on limiting patients' access to prescription drugs for legitimate medical needs. We analyzed survey responses and compared them to federal internal control standards related to information and communication and the standards in DEA's Office of Diversion Control Customer Service Plan for Registrants.[13]

To further address all three objectives, we interviewed government officials at 16 agencies within four states (California, Florida, Kentucky, and New York) and officials at 26 national associations to obtain information about interactions with DEA, their perspectives about those interactions, and their views about the effects of DEA enforcement actions on abuse and diversion and access to legitimate prescription medication. We selected these four states based on several criteria, including that they (1) have varied levels of prescription drug overdose deaths, (2) have received federal grant funds relevant to reducing prescription drug abuse and diversion, and (3) represented different geographic regions of the country (as represented by DEA field divisions). We interviewed officials at 16 state agencies within these four states, including state regulatory authorities such as pharmacy and medical boards, law enforcement, and agencies that oversee the state's prescription drug monitoring program. Although the perspectives we obtained during the interviews with state agencies and national associations are not generalizable, the interviews provided insights regarding how these types of entities interact with DEA as well as common areas of concern.

We also obtained documents from and interviewed DEA Office of Diversion Control officials who have oversight responsibility for DEA registrants and are engaged in addressing prescription drug abuse and diversion issues to learn about how DEA interacts with its registrants and other nonfederal stakeholders, and to obtain DEA's perspectives on information we obtained from our survey results and interviews with nonfederal stakeholders. In addition, in each of the four states where we conducted interviews with state agency officials, we also interviewed officials from DEA field divisions, such as supervisors overseeing both diversion investigators and special agents. We compared DEA's responses regarding its interactions with registrants and nonfederal stakeholders to federal internal control standards related to information and communication and the standards in DEA's Office of Diversion Control Customer Service Plan for Registrants.[14] Finally, to help address our third objective, we reviewed data on DEA's enforcement actions from fiscal year 2009 through fiscal year 2013 that were taken against DEA registrants in the three categories that we included in our surveys (distributors, pharmacies, and practitioners) to identify any trends in DEA's enforcement actions over a recent time period. We determined that the data were sufficiently reliable for purposes of our report. (See app. I for a detailed discussion of our scope and methodology.)

We conducted this performance audit from August 2013 to June 2015 in accordance with generally accepted government auditing standards. Those standards require that we plan and perform the audit to obtain sufficient, appropriate evidence to provide a reasonable basis for our findings and conclusions based on our audit objectives. We believe that the evidence obtained provides a reasonable basis for our findings and conclusions based on our audit objectives.

BACKGROUND

Prescription opioid pain relievers are safe and effective when used as directed, but these highly addictive substances can pose serious risks of addiction or death if they are abused, misused, or diverted. Opportunities for abuse or diversion can occur as drugs flow through the prescription drug supply chain. DEA is responsible for ensuring the availability of controlled substances for legitimate uses while preventing their diversion through its administration and enforcement of the CSA and its implementing regulations.[15] States also play a role in regulating controlled substances and the practices of medicine and pharmacy within their state boundaries. Additionally, national associations representing stakeholders such as distributors, pharmacies, and practitioners work on behalf of their members to support efforts to reduce prescription drug abuse and diversion.

Legitimate Use of Prescription Drugs, Drug Supply Chain, and Opportunities for Abuse and Diversion

When taken as directed for legitimate medical purposes, prescription drugs are safe and effective. Pain, which affects millions of Americans, is a health problem for which prescription drugs are often used. Pain can be characterized in terms of intensity—mild to severe—and duration—acute or chronic. According to the Institute of Medicine, more than 100 million Americans are affected by chronic pain.[16] While the appropriate medical treatment of pain varies, some patients are prescribed prescription pain relievers, such as opioids, to treat pain. These may include hydrocodone, oxycodone, and morphine, among other opioids. Prescription opioid pain relievers can be used effectively as a short-term treatment for a variety of acute or chronic pain conditions, such as severe pain following trauma, and for patients with painful terminal diseases such as cancer. However, opioids are sometimes used in a manner other than as prescribed—that is, they are abused and misused. Because opioids are highly addictive substances, they can pose serious risks when they are abused and misused, which can lead to addiction and cause death.

The prescription drug supply chain is the means through which prescription drugs are ultimately delivered to patients with legitimate medical needs. Although there can be many variations in the flow of prescription drugs through the supply chain, in a common example, prescription drugs are produced by manufacturers; are purchased and stored by distributors, who take orders and deliver them to customers such as pharmacies; and ultimately are dispensed by pharmacies to patients who have a prescription from a practitioner. (See figure 1.) Although prescription drugs are intended for legitimate medical uses, the prescription drug supply chain may present opportunities for the drugs to be abused and diverted as the drugs move through the various components of the supply chain. For example, an individual may visit multiple practitioners posing as a legitimate patient, referred to as a doctor shopper, to obtain prescriptions for drugs for themselves or others. In an example of diversion, criminal enterprises may rob distributors and pharmacies of prescription drugs to sell to others for a profit.

DEA's Office of Diversion Control and the CSA

Through its Office of Diversion Control, DEA administers the Diversion Control Program whose mission is to prevent, detect, and investigate the diversion of controlled substances from legitimate sources while ensuring an adequate and uninterrupted supply is available for legitimate medical, commercial, and scientific needs. In addition to investigations, the Office of Diversion Control conducts a variety of activities such as establishing quotas on the total amount of each basic class of controlled substance that can be manufactured, promulgating regulations for handling controlled substances, regulating handlers of controlled substances, and monitoring the production and distribution of certain controlled substances, among other things.[17]

The CSA requires businesses, entities, or individuals that import, export, manufacture, distribute, dispense, conduct research with respect to, or administer controlled substances to register with the DEA. As of December 2014, along with other registrants, there were over 1.5 million registered distributors, pharmacies, and practitioners. (See table 1.)

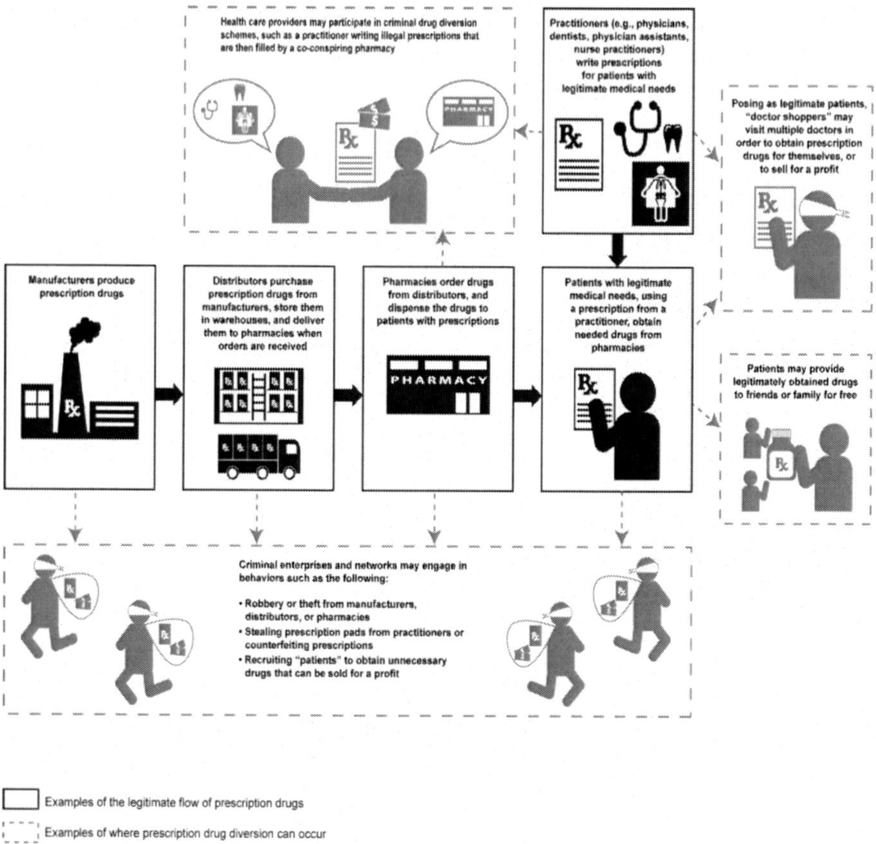

Source: GAO (data); GAO and Art Explosion (clipart). | GAO-15-471

Figure 1. An Example of the Prescription Drug Supply Chain and Opportunities for Abuse and Diversion.

Table 1. Numbers of Drug Enforcement Administration (DEA) Registrants, as of December 2014

DEA registrant type	Numbers	Percentage of total
Distributors	986	0.06
Pharmacies	70,387	4.51
Practitioners[a]	1,457,690	93.46
Other DEA registrants[b]	30,647	1.96
Total	**1,559,710**	**100**

Source: DEA. | GAO-15-471

[a] The category of practitioners, as summarized here, includes both those who DEA categorizes for registration purposes as practitioners (e.g., physicians, dentists, and podiatrists), and those who DEA categorizes for registration purposes as mid-level practitioners, such as nurse practitioners, nurse midwives, nurse anesthetists, clinical nurse specialists, and physician assistants.

[b] The category of other DEA registrants as summarized here includes registrants such as manufacturers, hospitals and clinics, importers/exporters of controlled substances, narcotic treatment programs, and researchers who use controlled substances or medications in their research or analyses.

DEA registrants must comply with a variety of requirements imposed by the CSA and its implementing regulations. For example, a registrant must keep accurate records and maintain inventories of controlled substances, among other requirements, in compliance with applicable federal and state laws. Additionally, all registrants must provide effective controls and procedures to guard against theft and diversion of controlled substances. Examples of some of the specific regulatory requirements for distributors, pharmacists, and practitioners include the following:

- **Distributors:** Registrants must design and operate a system to disclose suspicious orders of controlled substances, and must inform the DEA field division office in the registrant's area of suspicious orders when the registrant discovers them.[18]
- **Pharmacists:** While the responsibility for proper prescribing and dispensing of controlled substances rests with the prescribing practitioner, the pharmacist who fills the prescription holds a corresponding responsibility for ensuring that the prescription was issued in the usual course of professional treatment for a legitimate purpose.[19]
- **Practitioners:** Practitioners are responsible for the proper prescribing and dispensing of controlled substances for legitimate medical uses. A prescription for a controlled substance must be issued for a legitimate medical purpose by an individual practitioner acting in the usual course of that person's professional practice.[20]

As part of the registrant monitoring process and to ensure compliance with the CSA and its implementing regulations, DEA conducts three types of investigations—regulatory, complaint, and criminal.

- **Regulatory investigations:** DEA conducts different types of regulatory investigations, including scheduled, or cyclic, investigations (inspections) of DEA registrants.[21] Scheduled investigations are conducted at a frequency depending on the registrant's business activity, and occur every 2, 3 or 5 years. Registrants such as physicians—with the exception of physicians permitted to treat narcotic dependence—generally do not receive scheduled investigations by the DEA. These registrants may be regularly investigated by the states in which they conduct business.
- **Complaint investigations:** Complaint investigations are started on the basis of information or a tip provided to DEA or state regulators, or other information DEA has regarding the diversion of controlled substances. The origin of the information could be from any number of sources, such as a state or local official or citizen who observed something suspicious, employees of a registrant, the identification by DEA of unusual purchasing trends by a registrant such as a pharmacy that is tracked through DEA's Automation of Reports and Consolidated Orders System (ARCOS), or a report to DEA of a loss of controlled substances by a registrant.[22]
- **Criminal investigations:** DEA also conducts investigations into criminal activities involving diversion of controlled substances that may involve DEA registrants or nonregistrants, such as an undercover purchase of a controlled substance from an individual who is not a registrant.

Within its 21 field divisions, DEA utilizes a variety of personnel (including diversion investigators, special agents, and task force officers) to carry out these investigative responsibilities.

Following an investigation, DEA can initiate a variety of enforcement actions for violations of the CSA or its implementing regulations—administrative, civil, and criminal. The type(s) of action initiated is within DEA's discretion and is typically driven by the severity of the offense(s) and whether a registrant was the subject of any previous actions. The penalties associated with different enforcement actions likewise vary in severity.

- **Administrative actions:** Administrative actions are handled primarily by DEA and can include (1) a letter of admonition to advise the registrant of any violations and necessary corrective action, (2) a memorandum of agreement which outlines things the registrants agree to do to become compliant and obligations of DEA when violations are corrected or not corrected, (3) an order to show cause that can initiate revocation or suspension of a DEA registration, and (4) an immediate suspension order that is issued when violations pose an imminent threat to public health or safety, and deprive the registrant of the ability to handle controlled substances upon service of the suspension order.

- **Civil penalties:** Civil penalties generally include monetary fines.
- **Criminal penalties:** Criminal penalties generally include incarceration and fines.

States' Roles in the Regulation of Controlled Substances and Health Care

Each state has a role in regulating controlled substances and health care within its jurisdiction. For example, as of December 2014, 49 states and one U.S. territory (Guam) have operational prescription drug monitoring programs, which collect data from dispensers and report information to authorized users, including practitioners and pharmacists.[23] Prescription drug monitoring program information can assist law enforcement and health care providers such as practitioners and pharmacists in identifying patterns of prescribing, dispensing, or receiving controlled substances that may indicate abuse or diversion. State prescription drug monitoring programs vary in numerous ways, including what information they collect; what drugs they cover; who has access to, or who is required to use, the prescription drug monitoring program; and which state agency oversees and administers the program.

States also govern the use of controlled substances through their own state controlled substances acts, and through the regulation of the practices of medicine and pharmacy. In general, to legally dispense a prescription drug, a pharmacist licensed by the state and working in a pharmacy licensed by the state must be presented a valid prescription from a licensed practitioner. The regulation of the practice of pharmacy is rooted in state pharmacy practice acts and regulations enforced by state boards of pharmacy. The state boards of pharmacy also are responsible for routinely inspecting pharmacies, ensuring that pharmacists and pharmacies comply with applicable laws, and investigating and disciplining those that fail to comply. All states also require that physicians practicing in the state be licensed to do so and state medical practice laws generally outline standards for the practice of medicine and delegate the responsibility of regulating physicians to state medical boards. Each state's medical board also defines the elements of a valid patient-provider relationship, and grants prescribing privileges to physicians and other practitioners.[24]

National Associations' Roles in Efforts to Reduce Prescription Drug Abuse and Diversion

National associations also play a role in efforts to reduce prescription drug abuse and diversion. National associations represent the interests of their members or constituents, which can include DEA registrants, such as pharmacies, practitioners, and distributors; various state governmental agencies or employees, such as state regulatory boards and law enforcement entities; and patient groups, among others. These national associations may support their members in various ways, such as providing guidance and training to help educate members about abuse and diversion; commenting on proposed legislation, such as proper disposal of prescription drugs; and lobbying on behalf of their members or constituents to federal agencies and members of Congress.

Registrants Vary in Extent of Interaction with DEA and Awareness of DEA Resources, and While Generally Satisfied, Some Want Additional Information

Results from our generalizable surveys of DEA registrants show that the extent of registrants' interaction with DEA varies. Our survey results also show that many registrants are not aware of DEA conferences and resources. Of those registrants that reported that they had interacted with DEA since January 1, 2012, most were generally satisfied. However, some distributors, individual pharmacies, and chain pharmacy corporate offices reported that they want additional guidance from, and communication with, DEA.

Registrants Interact with DEA through Several Methods, but to Different Extents, and Many Are Not Aware of DEA Conferences and Resources

We surveyed registrants about three primary methods for interacting with DEA—direct communication with DEA headquarters or field office staff; participation in DEA conferences, initiatives, or training; and utilization of DEA resources, such as guidance. Our survey results show that registrants interact with DEA through these methods to varying degrees, and that many registrants are not aware of DEA conferences and resources.

Table 2. Drug Enforcement Administration (DEA) Registrants That Have Communicated with DEA Headquarters or Field Office Staff

Type of interaction	Distributors	Individual pharmacies	Chain pharmacy corporate offices[a]	Practitioners
Communicated with DEA headquarters staff	n/a	28%	59% (19)	12%
Communicated with DEA field office staff	n/a	24%	84% (27)	8%
Communicated with DEA headquarters staff or a DEA field office	81%	n/a	n/a	n/a

Source: GAO surveys of DEA registrants. | GAO-15-471

Notes: Between July 2014 and October 2014, we surveyed generalizable random samples of DEA- registered distributors, individual pharmacies, and practitioners, and we surveyed all of the corporate offices of the 38 chain pharmacies we identified using a DEA database. Distributors were asked whether, since January 1, 2012, they had any communications (outside of conferences, initiatives, or training) with DEA headquarters or field office staff about their Controlled Substances Act roles and responsibilities. Individual pharmacies, chain pharmacy corporate offices, and practitioners were asked two separate versions of this question—one specific to DEA headquarters staff, and one specific to DEA field office staff. Percentage estimates for distributors, individual pharmacies, and practitioners are subject to margins of error of no more than ±10 percentage points. An "n/a" indicates that the question was not offered to that registrant type.

[a] Responses are from the 32 chain pharmacy corporate offices that responded to our survey. We report both percentages and numbers (in parentheses) for the chain pharmacy corporate office responses because of the small population size.

Communication with DEA Headquarters or Field Office Staff

Based on our surveys, we found that the most common type of interaction between DEA and its registrants is direct communication with DEA headquarters or field office staff about registrants' roles and responsibilities under the CSA.[25] Most distributors and chain pharmacy corporate offices communicate with DEA headquarters or field office staff, while few individual pharmacies or practitioners do so. (See table 2.)[26] Registrants that reported that they had no communication with DEA headquarters or field office staff (outside of conferences, initiatives, or training) were asked to explain why not. Of those that offered a response, one common explanation was that the registrant did not feel any communication was necessary.

Of those registrants that had communicated with DEA headquarters or field office staff, the frequency of communication was typically less than once a quarter, although we estimate that some distributors (22 percent) and some chain pharmacy corporate offices (22 percent or 6 of 27) have communicated with DEA field office staff at least once a month since January 1, 2012. (See app. II, tables 12 and 13, for a complete listing of the numbers of registrants reporting various frequencies of communication with DEA headquarters and field office staff.) We did not survey registrants about the content of these communications with DEA headquarters or field office staff. However, the responses distributors, chain pharmacy corporate offices, and individual pharmacies offered to open-ended questions in these sections of our surveys suggest that the substance of this communication is wide ranging. For example, registrants cited communication with DEA ranging from inquiries about regulatory responsibilities to questions about suspicious customers and reporting of thefts. The most common methods of communication reported across registrant types generally were telephone or e-mail communication, although we estimate that most distributors (76 percent) also have in-person communication with DEA field office staff. (See app. II, table 14, for a complete listing of numbers of registrants reporting various methods of communication with DEA headquarters and field office staff.)

The reasons for greater communication with DEA among distributors and chain pharmacy corporate offices may be related to the nature of their relationship with DEA. For example, distributors are required to renew their DEA registration annually, and are subject to scheduled, cyclical regulatory investigations. Conversely, pharmacies and practitioners only have to renew their DEA registration every three years, and are not subject to scheduled, cyclical regulatory investigations. Because the chain pharmacy corporate offices we surveyed represent 50 or more individual pharmacies, it follows that they might have more regular communication with DEA on behalf of those pharmacies.

Participation in Conferences, Initiatives, or Training

Results from our surveys show that smaller percentages of DEA registrants have interacted with DEA via conferences, initiatives, or training (see table 3), although many registrants are not aware of these opportunities.

Table 3. Drug Enforcement Administration (DEA) Registrants That Participated in Conferences, Initiatives, or Training Offered by DEA

Type of interaction	Distributors	Individual pharmacies	Chain pharmacy corporate offices[a]	Practitioners
October 2013 Distributor Conference	27%	n/a	n/a	n/a
Distributor Initiative briefing	12%	n/a	n/a	n/a
Pharmacy Diversion Awareness Conferences (PDAC)	n/a	17%	63% (20)	n/a
Other DEA conferences, initiatives, or training	19%	8%	31% (10)	7%

Source: GAO surveys of DEA registrants. | GAO-15-471

Notes: Between July 2014 and October 2014, we surveyed generalizable random samples of DEA- registered distributors, individual pharmacies, and practitioners, and we surveyed all of the corporate offices of the 38 chain pharmacies we identified using a DEA database. Registrants were asked variations of questions specific to their registrant type about whether, since January 1, 2012, they had participated in the DEA-offered conferences, initiatives, or training listed above. Percentage estimates for distributors, individual pharmacies, and practitioners are subject to margins of error of no more than ±10 percentage points. An "n/a" indicates that the question or response was not offered to that registrant type.

[a] Responses are from the 32 chain pharmacy corporate offices that responded to our survey. We report both percentages and numbers (in parentheses) for the chain pharmacy corporate office responses because of the small population size.

DEA periodically hosts events such as conferences or meetings for various components of its registrant population during which the agency provides information about registrants' CSA roles and responsibilities for preventing abuse and diversion. DEA is also often a presenter at various conferences at the national, state, or local level, which registrants may attend. DEA places information about upcoming conferences that it is hosting on its website, and DEA officials said that to further publicize them DEA has sent emails or letters to registrants about these events, but also relies on state regulatory boards and national associations to promote them.[27] Distributors were asked whether representatives of their facility attended DEA's 2013 Distributor Conference, and individual pharmacies and chain pharmacy corporate offices were asked whether they or other representatives of their pharmacy (or pharmacy chain) had attended a Pharmacy Diversion Awareness Conference (PDAC).[28]

Based on our surveys, we estimate that 27 percent of distributors and 17 percent of individual pharmacies have participated in the DEA-hosted events, while 63 percent (20 of 32) of chain pharmacy corporate offices we surveyed had participated in a PDAC. Of the large percentages of distributors and pharmacies that did not participate in these conferences, many cited lack of awareness as the reason. For example, an estimated 76 percent of individual pharmacies that had not attended a PDAC and 35 percent of distributors that had not attended the 2013 Distributor Conference cited lack of awareness as a reason for not participating.[29] (See app. II, table 15 and table 16, for additional reasons reported by distributors and pharmacies for not participating in these conferences.) While it is possible that some individual pharmacies are not aware of PDACs because one has not yet been scheduled or publicized in its state, the 76 percent of individual pharmacies that cite lack of awareness as a reason for not participating is a matter of concern since PDACs have been held in 21 states since 2011.

Some distributors have also interacted with DEA through its Distributor Initiative briefings, which are intended to educate and inform distributors of their responsibilities under the CSA.[30] Although only an estimated 12 percent of distributor facilities reported participating in these briefings since January 1, 2012, of those that reported that they had not attended, an estimated 12 percent said that a briefing had been attended by corporate or other company staff, and 4 percent said they participated in a briefing prior to 2012. (See app. II, table 15, for additional reasons distributors reported for not participating in these briefings.)

Table 4. Registrant Awareness of Various Drug Enforcement Administration (DEA) Resources

	DEA resource	Aware	Not aware	Don't know
Distributors	DEA's Know Your Customer guidance	51%	41%	8%
	DEA's registration validation tool	78%	17%	5%
Individual pharmacies	DEA's Pharmacist's Manual	42%	53%	6%
	DEA's registration validation tool	44%	53%	4%
Chain pharmacy corporate offices[a]	DEA's Pharmacist's Manual	69% (22)	31% (10)	0% (0)
	DEA's registration validation tool	78% (25)	19% (6)	3%(1)
Practitioners	DEA's Practitioner's Manual	20%	70%	10%

Source: GAO surveys of DEA registrants. | GAO-15-471

Notes: Between July 2014 and October 2014, we surveyed generalizable random samples of DEA-registered distributors, individual pharmacies, and practitioners, and we surveyed all of the corporate offices of the 38 chain pharmacies we identified using a DEA database. Registrants were asked variations of questions specific to their registrant type about whether they were aware of the specific DEA resource prior to receiving our survey questionnaire. Percentage estimates for distributors, individual pharmacies, and practitioners are subject to margins of error of no more than ±10 percentage points. Percentages may not add to 100 percent because of rounding.

[a] Responses are from the 32 chain pharmacy corporate offices that responded to our survey. We report both percentages and numbers (in parentheses) for the chain pharmacy corporate office responses because of the small population size.

We also asked all registrants whether they had participated in any other DEA conferences, initiatives, or training since January 1, 2012, and small percentages of registrants indicated that they had done so. (See table 3.) In the open-ended responses offered about the other DEA events they had attended, registrants across all four surveys cited, for example, DEA presentations at various professional association conferences or meetings they had attended.

Utilization of DEA Resources

DEA also has created various resources, such as guidance manuals and a registration validation tool, which registrants may utilize to understand or meet their roles and responsibilities under the CSA; however, based on our surveys, we found that many registrants are not utilizing these resources because they are not aware that they exist. (See table 4.) For example, DEA has created guidance manuals for pharmacists and practitioners to help them understand how the CSA and its implementing regulations pertain to these registrants' professions. These documents are available on DEA's Office of Diversion Control's website. In terms of guidance for distributors, in 2011 DEA released a document containing suggested questions a distributor should ask customers prior to shipping controlled substances (referred to as the Know Your Customer guidance). Additionally, DEA offers a registration validation tool on its website so that registrants, such as distributors and pharmacies, can determine if a pharmacy or practitioner has a valid, current DEA registration.

However, as shown in table 4, our survey results suggest that many registrants are not utilizing these resources that could help them better understand and meet their CSA roles and responsibilities because they are unfamiliar with them. For example, of particular concern are the estimated 53 percent of individual pharmacies that are not aware of either DEA's Pharmacist's Manual or the registration validation tool, and the 70 percent of practitioners that are not aware of DEA's Practitioner's Manual, and are therefore not utilizing these resources.

In addition to the resources listed above, we also asked registrants whether there were "any other DEA guidance, resources, or tools (e.g. DEA's Office of Diversion Control website or DEA presentations available online)" that they had used to understand their roles and responsibilities. We estimate that while nearly half of distributors (42 percent) and chain pharmacy corporate offices (47 percent or 15 of 32) have used other DEA resources, only small percentages of individual pharmacies (15 percent) or practitioners (7 percent) have done so. Of those distributors and chain pharmacy corporate offices that offered responses about what other DEA resources they have used, usage of DEA's website was the most common response, with some distributors noting that they also refer to published DEA regulations, and some chain pharmacy corporate offices noting that they have referred to presentations from past DEA conferences.

The lack of awareness among registrants of DEA resources and conferences suggests that DEA may not have an adequate means of communicating with its registrant populations. While DEA's website contains information and links for specific guidance, tools, and conferences, if registrants are unaware that these types of resources exist, they will not know to search DEA's website for them. And although DEA officials told us that many registrants should be familiar with DEA's website because that is where they renew their registration, a DEA official estimated that about 14 percent of registrants register by paper, and registration renewal is only required once every three years for pharmacies and practitioners. Also, many of the registrants we surveyed reported that they had not used other DEA resources such as DEA's website to understand their roles and responsibilities under the CSA. For example, we estimate that 69 percent of individual pharmacies and 46 percent of distributors have not used other DEA resources such as DEA's website for this purpose. Therefore, while most registrants are using DEA's website to renew their registration, it is likely that registrants responding to our survey did not consider this usage of DEA's website an activity that helped them understand their CSA roles and responsibilities.

Furthermore, while DEA has promoted some conferences via email, the agency does not have current, valid email addresses for all of its registrants. DEA reports that email addresses are not required information for registrants, and that mailed correspondence to a registrant's address is the official method of communication. A DEA official told us that while DEA has email addresses for the approximately 86 percent of registrants that renew their registration online, not all of these email addresses may be current or valid. For example, the official noted that because pharmacies and practitioners are only required to renew their registration every three years, the email addresses for those groups may be less accurate, as the registrant's email address may have changed during that time.

The standards in DEA's Office of Diversion Control Customer Service Plan for Registrants state that DEA will provide guidance regarding the CSA and its regulations. Additionally, federal internal control standards state that management should ensure there are adequate means of communicating with stakeholders who may have a significant impact on the agency achieving its goals.[31] Despite the lack of awareness we found that existed among registrants, DEA officials have indicated that they do not believe they need to take any additional steps to improve communication or raise registrants' awareness of the agency's conferences and resources.

Other federal agencies use practices that may be useful to DEA to increase registrants' awareness of agency resources. For example, an additional method for communicating with stakeholders that other federal agencies, such as the Centers for Medicare & Medicaid Services (CMS) and National Institutes of

Health, have used is a listserv—an electronic mailing list through which external stakeholders sign up to receive information on various topics of interest. For example, the bottom right corner of any page on CMS.gov has a link through which interested parties can sign up to receive e-mail updates from CMS on a wide variety of topics. DEA could examine the use of these or other communication methods to help keep relevant registrant populations informed about upcoming conferences, new or revised resources, or other materials or activities that inform registrants about their responsibilities regarding the CSA and its implementing regulations.

With so many registrants unaware of DEA's conferences and resources, DEA lacks assurance that registrants have sufficient information to understand and meet their CSA responsibilities. If registrants do not meet their CSA responsibilities, they could be subject to DEA enforcement actions. However, since DEA officials reported that the agency's goal is to bring registrants into compliance rather than take enforcement actions against them, additional communication with registrants about DEA's conferences and resources may help the agency better achieve this goal.

Most Registrants that Interacted with DEA are Generally Satisfied, Although Some Distributors and Pharmacies Want Additional Communication and Guidance

Most Registrants That Interacted with DEA Were Generally Satisfied

Our survey results showed that while many registrants, particularly individual pharmacies and practitioners, did not report any interaction with DEA since 2012, most of those that did interact with DEA were generally positive about those interactions. For example, of the registrants that communicated with DEA headquarters or field office staff, most reported that the communication was very or moderately helpful. (See table 5.) Distributors that communicated with DEA field offices about their roles and responsibilities under the CSA were particularly satisfied—we estimate that 92 percent of distributors found the field office staff very or moderately helpful. However, some registrants reported dissatisfaction with DEA communication. For example, 6 of 26 chain pharmacy corporate offices that reported communicating with DEA field offices said that staff were slightly or not at all helpful.

Table 5. Numbers of Registrants Reporting Perspectives on the Helpfulness of Communication with Drug Enforcement Administration (DEA) Headquarters or Field Office Staff

	Type of respondent	Very or moderately helpful	Slightly or not at all helpful	Don't know	Not applicable – no inquiries	Total responses
DEA headquarters staff	Distributors	43	10	3	50	**106**
	Individual pharmacies	30	7	8	n/a	**45**
	Chain pharmacy corporate offices	14	4	1	n/a	**19**
	Practitioners	9	2	8	n/a	**19**
DEA field office staff	Distributors	109	9	0	1	**119**
	Individual pharmacies	29	6	4	n/a	**39**
	Chain pharmacy corporate offices	20	6	0	n/a	**26**
	Practitioners	7	2	4	n/a	**13**

Source: GAO surveys of DEA registrants. | GAO-15-471

Notes: Between July 2014 and October 2014, we surveyed generalizable random samples of DEA- registered distributors, individual pharmacies, and practitioners, and we surveyed all of the corporate offices of the 38 chain pharmacies we identified using a DEA database. Registrants were asked variations of a question specific to their registrant type about, in general, how helpful DEA headquarters and field office staff have been to registrants' inquiries about their roles and responsibilities. An "n/a" indicates that the response choice was not offered to that registrant type.

Similarly, when asked about DEA's performance relative to certain customer service standards, most of the registrants that reported communicating with DEA headquarters or field office staff were positive about their interactions with staff. DEA's Office of Diversion Control Customer Service Plan for Registrants has standards for interacting with registrants, which include the following expectations:

- Courteous and professional treatment from DEA personnel;
- Responses to: written, electronic, or telephone inquiries; concerns and criticisms; and complaints and suggestions to improve DEA service, procedures, and performance; and
- Discretion in handling sensitive information.

When asked about their interactions with DEA relative to these standards, generally most registrants that communicated with DEA headquarters or field office staff reported that staff were very or moderately responsive, very or moderately courteous and respectful, and showed great or moderate discretion when handling sensitive information. For example, we estimate that 93 percent of distributors and 77 percent of individual pharmacies found DEA field office staff very or moderately responsive to their inquiries.[32] (See app. II, table 17 through table 19, for a complete listing of the number of registrants reporting perspectives on both DEA headquarters and field office staff on these three standards.) Ratings were similarly positive for both DEA headquarters and field office staff, although distributors and chain pharmacy corporate offices more often reported having made inquiries to DEA field office staff than DEA headquarters staff.

Finally, related to DEA conferences, initiatives, or training, while most registrants other than chain pharmacy corporate offices had not attended such events, the most frequent response among registrants that reported attending was that these events were very or moderately helpful for understanding their CSA roles and responsibilities. (See app. II, table 20.)

"DEA conferences and training are extremely helpful. I've been told by other participants it brings value and gives guidance to pharmacies to ensure they are doing things properly."

Source: GAO chain pharmacy corporate office survey. | GAO-15-471

For example, most of the individual pharmacies and chain pharmacy corporate offices that reported attending one of DEA's PDACs found them very or moderately helpful. Similarly, many distributors (29 of 40) that reported attending DEA's October 2013 Distributor Conference said that it was very or moderately helpful, although a smaller but notable number of distributors (11 of 40) that attended reported that the conference was slightly or not at all helpful. Criticisms of the 2013 Distributor Conference that were offered by distributors in their open-ended responses included the presentation of outdated or previously shared information, and that the information shared was too general and did not provide the specific guidance registrants were expecting.

Some Distributors Want Additional Guidance and More Communication

Some survey responses indicate that additional guidance for distributors regarding suspicious orders monitoring and reporting, as well as more regular communication, would be beneficial. For example, while DEA has created guidance manuals for pharmacists and practitioners, the agency has not developed a guidance manual or comparable document for distributors. As noted previously, standards in DEA's Customer Service Plan for Registrants include providing guidance regarding the CSA and its regulations, and internal control standards for federal agencies state that management should ensure there are adequate means of communicating with stakeholders that may have a significant impact on the agency achieving its goals.[33]

"It would be very helpful, if DEA provided further clarification regarding responsibilities associated with 21 CFR 1301.74(b), [Suspicious] Order Monitoring and applicable guidance letters. DEA has pursued aggressive enforcement of these regulations, but [does] not provide a clear roadmap for what is expected to be compliant. Also, vague mandates of 'knowing your customers' needs to be clarified as it [cannot] be found within the CFR or guidance [letters]...It would also be very beneficial for industry if DEA would schedule a periodic (perhaps quarterly) briefing, via web meeting, or similar technology, to inform industry of trends that they are seeing; drugs of abuse, geographic areas, etc., so that we can work proactively as partners in prevention of diversion and abuse...DEA is comprised of many dedicated professionals that have a great deal of information that can be shared, but it needs to be ongoing and inclusive, not every other year or two at a seminar. Combined, industry and DEA can have a big impact."

Source: GAO distributor survey. | GAO-15-471

In response to an open-ended question in our survey about how DEA could improve its Know Your Customer document, the guidance document DEA has provided to distributors, half of distributors (28 of 55) that offered comments said that they want more guidance from DEA. Additionally, just over one-third of distributors (28 of 77) reported that DEA's Know Your Customer document was slightly or not at all helpful.[34] (See app. II, table 21 for a complete listing of registrant responses on the helpfulness of various DEA resources.) Furthermore, in response to an open-ended question about what additional interactions they would find helpful to have with DEA, more than half of the distributors that offered comments (36 of 55) said that they needed more communication or information from, or interactions with, DEA. Some of the specific comments noted that distributors would like more proactive communication from DEA that is collaborative in nature, rather than being solely violation- or enforcement-oriented. Some of the additional communication and interactions proposed by distributors included quarterly meetings with the local field office and more training or conferences related to their regulatory roles and responsibilities.

DEA officials told us that they believe the information in agency regulations is sufficient for distributors to understand their CSA responsibilities for suspicious orders monitoring and reporting. DEA officials said that they have not created guidance manuals for distributors similar to what they have done for pharmacies and practitioners because they meet routinely with distributors and distributors have fewer requirements compared to those other registrant types and officials don't believe such guidance is necessary. Additionally, DEA officials said that while distributors want specific instructions on how to avoid enforcement actions, DEA cannot do that because circumstances that lead to enforcement actions (e.g., individual business practices) vary. DEA officials said that distributors must make informed business decisions regarding customers that are diverting prescription drugs, and that DEA cannot tell distributors not to ship to specific customers. Officials told us that they would advise distributors to know their customers and their typical orders so that they'll be able to identify unusual or suspicious orders or purchasers. DEA officials also suggested that distributors should refer to the enforcement actions against distributors that are described on DEA's website in order to learn "what not to do." Regarding their communication with registrants, DEA officials also indicated that they do not think they need to make any changes in their practices. They said that they believe that they are accessible to any registrant, and that registrants can contact either DEA headquarters or field office staff if they have questions.

"... if DEA would provide specific metrics of 'normal' pharmacies based on overall prescription volume and/or a set of 'safe harbor' standards for distributors, supply disruptions would be minimized."

Source: GAO chain pharmacy corporate office survey. | GAO-15-471

A guidance document for distributors similar to the one offered for pharmacies and practitioners could help distributors further understand and meet their roles and responsibilities under the CSA for preventing diversion, though the document may not need to be as detailed. Specifically, although DEA may not be able to provide guidance that will definitively answer the question of what constitutes a suspicious order or offer advice about which customers to ship to, DEA could, for example, provide guidance around best practices in developing suspicious orders monitoring systems. DEA could also enhance its proactive communication with distributors—which could be done, for example, via electronic means if additional in-person outreach would be cost prohibitive. Such steps are key to addressing distributors' concerns, as without sufficient guidance and communication from DEA, distributors may not be fully understanding or meeting their roles and responsibilities under the CSA for preventing diversion. Additionally, in the absence of clear guidance from DEA, our survey data show that many distributors are setting thresholds on the amount of certain controlled substances that can be ordered by their customers (i.e., pharmacies and practitioners), which can negatively impact pharmacies and ultimately patients' access. For example, we estimate that 62 percent of individual pharmacies do business with distributors that put thresholds on the quantity of controlled substances they can order, and we estimate that 25 percent of individual pharmacies have had orders cancelled or suspended by distributors.

Some Pharmacies Want Improved Guidance and More Communication from DEA

Responses to our surveys also show that some pharmacies want updated or clearer guidance, as well as more communication and information, from DEA. The agency has provided a guidance manual for pharmacists, and of the pharmacies that were aware of DEA's Pharmacist's Manual, most said that it was helpful. For example, most individual pharmacies (54 of 68) that were aware of the manual found it very or moderately helpful. (See app. II, table 21.) However, DEA's Pharmacist's Manual was last updated in 2010, and since that time DEA has levied large civil fines against some pharmacies; some pharmacy associations reported these fines have caused confusion in the industry about pharmacists' CSA roles and responsibilities. As noted previously, DEA's customer service plan standards call for the agency to provide guidance regarding the CSA and its regulations, and federal internal control standards call for adequate communication channels with stakeholders.[35] In their responses to an open-ended question in our survey about DEA's Pharmacist's Manual, some chain pharmacy corporate offices (7 of 18) said that the manual needed updates or more detail, some chain pharmacy corporate offices (5 of 18) reported other concerns with the manual, and some individual pharmacies (13 of 33) said that the manual needed improvement, such as more specifics. For example, several chain pharmacy corporate offices commented that the manual needed to be updated to reflect changes in DEA enforcement practices or regulations (e.g., the rescheduling of hydrocodone from a schedule III to a schedule II drug).[36]

The need for clearer guidance for pharmacists was also suggested by some chain pharmacy corporate offices' responses to a question about DEA field office consistency. Specifically, when asked how consistent the responses of staff in different field offices have been to their inquiries about pharmacists' roles and responsibilities, nearly half of chain pharmacy corporate offices (8 of 19) that had contact with multiple DEA field offices said that staff responses were slightly or not at all consistent. (See app. II, table 22.) In an open-ended response to this question, one chain pharmacy corporate office noted that in its interactions with different DEA field offices throughout the country it has received different, widely varying interpretations of DEA requirements that affect the chain's day-to- day operations, such as requirements for theft/loss reporting of controlled substances and requirements for prescribers to be reported when the prescriber fails to provide a written prescription. These responses from chain pharmacy corporate offices about field office inconsistencies suggest that the existing pharmacy guidance may not be clear even to some DEA field office officials.

Additionally, the desire for more or clearer guidance and more communication from DEA was a common theme in the responses offered from both individual pharmacies and chain pharmacy corporate offices to the open-ended questions in our survey related to DEA interactions. For example, in response to an open-ended question about what additional interactions they would find helpful to have with DEA headquarters or field office staff, nearly all of the chain pharmacy corporate offices that offered comments (15 of 18) said that they wanted more guidance or clearer interpretation of the guidance from DEA, more communication with DEA, or a more proactive, collaborative relationship with DEA. In addition, nearly a third of individual pharmacies (18 of 60) that offered open-ended answers to a question about any new guidance, resources, or tools that DEA should provide to help them understand their roles and responsibilities said that they would like more proactive communication from DEA through methods such as a newsletter or e-mail blast. Some chain pharmacy corporate offices (7 of 17) and individual pharmacies (11 of 33) also offered comments expressing a desire to receive up-to-date information on data or trends in diversion of prescription drugs from DEA. The majority of pharmacy registrants that reported having seen DEA data on trends in prescription drug abuse and diversion found the information to be very or moderately helpful for understanding how to identify common abuse and diversion tactics (43 of 57 individual pharmacies and 23 of 25 chain pharmacy corporate offices), suggesting that information of this kind could be very helpful to pharmacy registrants if it was more widely distributed. (See app. II, table 21.)

"The DEA has NO communication out to pharmacies at all. The DEA is not preventive, it is all reactive. The only experience we get with the DEA is hearing when they investigate and levy fines against a pharmacy for common pharmacy practices. [Expectations] and guidelines regarding rules are unclear. It would be much more helpful for the DEA to work on a preventative approach by more communication, outreach, and clear expectations. This would help everyone involved while increasing public safety."

Source: GAO individual pharmacy survey. | GAO-15-471

However, DEA officials indicated that they do not believe there is a need for additional guidance for or communication with pharmacy registrants, and that the current methods by which the agency helps pharmacy registrants understand their CSA roles and responsibilities are sufficient. DEA officials said that registrants can write, call, or e-mail DEA headquarters or field offices if they have questions. Officials also said that the agency has reached out to pharmacy registrants via their PDACs; however, because DEA had held only 44 PDACs in 21 states between 2011 and 2014, many pharmacy registrants had not had the opportunity to attend these conferences. Additionally, in their open-ended responses to questions in the section of our survey about DEA conferences, several individual pharmacies also cited their distance from the cities in which training is often held as their reason for not attending, with one individual pharmacy suggesting that a web-based training option would be helpful.

Regarding the concern about inconsistencies in responses among DEA field offices related to inquiries about pharmacies' roles and responsibilities under the CSA, DEA headquarters officials said that they have heard this concern in the past, but when they ask for specific examples of the conflicting information, registrants do not provide specific, actionable details. DEA officials acknowledged that interpretations can vary among different investigators and said that they have provided training to their staff to ensure consistent interpretation of regulations, including an annual conference and training of every diversion investigator, to address this concern.

> "I think we would have liked to have had more proactive engagement [with DEA]. Particularly as pharmacy chains came together and tried to bring forward model best practices. Because of [DEA's] enforcement approach, we have pushed hard to ensure that if a pharmacist questions the legitimacy of a script, decline to fill. This is a position that Boards of Pharmacy have stated is not in the best interests of patients. We specifically requested [Boards of Pharmacy] work with the DEA to reconcile their views. This puts pharmacists in a very difficult predicament and if in doubt, they will decline to fill."
>
> Source: GAO chain pharmacy corporate office survey. | GAO-15-471

As indicated in the concerns expressed by some pharmacy registrants, without clear guidance or adequate communication with and information from DEA, these registrants may not fully understand or meet their responsibilities for preventing abuse and diversion under the CSA. Furthermore, without adequate communication with pharmacy registrants, DEA may not fully understand registrants' needs and how best to address them. Additionally, in the absence of clear guidance from DEA, some pharmacies may be inappropriately delaying or denying filling prescriptions for patients with legitimate medical needs. For example, we estimate that 22 percent of practitioners have had pharmacies delay filling the prescriptions they wrote, and 13 percent of practitioners have had pharmacies deny filling certain prescriptions for controlled substances.

State Agencies and National Associations Interact with DEA through Joint Task Forces or Meetings, and While Generally Satisfied, Some Associations Want Improved Communication

Officials from state agencies we interviewed told us that they interact with DEA through law enforcement activities, such as joint task forces, and other activities, while officials from national associations we interviewed said that they most often interact with DEA by hosting and participating in meetings. Nearly all state agencies and more than half of the national associations told us that they were generally satisfied with their interactions with DEA; however, some national associations wanted improved communication with DEA.

State Agencies Interact with DEA through Law Enforcement Activities, Attending Joint Events, and Sharing Data, and Nearly All were Satisfied with their Interactions

Among the 16 state agencies we interviewed, 14 reported interacting with DEA, most commonly through law enforcement activities (including joint task forces, investigations, and inspections), meetings and presentations, and sharing prescription drug monitoring program and other types of data to help reduce prescription drug abuse and diversion. Nearly all state agencies that reported interacting with DEA indicated that they were satisfied with those interactions.

Methods of Interaction with DEA

Of the 14 state agencies that interacted with DEA, the most common method reported to us was through law enforcement-related activities such as working together during investigations, or collaborating on joint task forces to reduce prescription drug abuse and diversion (11 of 14). For example, officials from a state medical board reported that the board collaborated with DEA on an investigation against a physician involving fraud and questionable prescribing practices which resulted in several patients' deaths. Additionally, officials from eight state agencies we interviewed reported working with DEA and other law enforcement agencies in a task force setting such as with DEA Tactical Diversion Squads to investigate criminal prescription drug diversion cases.[37]

Most of the state agencies (11 of 14) also reported interacting with DEA through attending the same conferences, meetings, presentations, or workshops related to reducing prescription drug abuse and diversion. Specifically, officials from three state agencies reported that they invited DEA to present at an agency meeting; officials from another three state agencies reported that they were invited to speak at DEA sponsored events; and officials from three more state agencies reported they held general meetings with DEA to discuss trends and best practices. Officials from three state agencies also reported that their agencies jointly hosted a conference related to prescription drug abuse and diversion with DEA. Officials from some of the boards of pharmacy we interviewed reported that their boards collaborated with DEA on the agency's PDACs, such as by sending emails about the PDACs to their pharmacists to encourage participation, and by joining DEA in presentations about pharmacists' corresponding responsibilities.

More than half of the state agencies (9 of 14) reported interacting with DEA through sharing data, including sharing state prescription drug monitoring program data and other data about suspicious prescribers, pharmacies, or distributors. For example, an official from one state prescription drug monitoring program noted that the program responded to a request from DEA for its data related to a physician's prescribing history in order to support DEA's investigation into a prescription fraud ring in which the physician's DEA registration number had been used. Another state agency official reported that DEA shares its registrant information with the state agency when information is needed for investigative purposes.

A few state agencies (4 of 14) reported interacting with DEA through promoting DEA's prescription drug take-back events. According to DEA, the purpose of its National Take-Back events is to provide a safe, convenient, and responsible means of disposing prescription drugs, while educating the public about the potential for abuse and diversion of controlled substances.[38] DEA has partnered with others such as state and local law enforcement agencies to help with their take-back events. For example, officials from one state agency reported that they conduct outreach among local agencies about DEA's prescription drug take-back days and encourage participation from drug task forces in their state. Furthermore, officials representing a state board of pharmacy and a state law enforcement agency reported that they posted information about DEA's take-back events on their website, including locations collecting the unwanted, unused medications.

Satisfaction with DEA Interactions

Nearly all state agencies (13 of 14) that reported interacting with DEA indicated that they were satisfied with those interactions. For example, officials at some state agencies who reported that they participated in DEA's Tactical Diversion Squads or other investigative activities with DEA found those interactions to be positive and helpful—particularly as DEA provided access to additional investigative tools and resources and intelligence they would not otherwise have had access to. Furthermore, four state agencies we interviewed stated that they are easily able to exchange information or data with DEA, and officials have no problems in communicating and collaborating with DEA. Officials from two state agencies noted that they meet with DEA on a monthly or quarterly basis for presentations and to discuss updated information. Officials said that during these meetings they exchange recommendations and best practices for how to reduce prescription drug abuse and diversion. Furthermore, officials from two state agencies—both pharmacy boards—reported that DEA's education outreach efforts through its PDACs were positive and provided invaluable information. Officials from one state board suggested that because the PDACs held in their state have been so valuable, pharmacists should be required to attend these conferences, and that they would encourage DEA to offer more PDACs in their state.

One state board reported dissatisfaction with its interactions with DEA related to DEA enforcement actions against pharmacists in the state, and differences in how DEA field office staff and the state pharmacy board interpret laws and regulations affecting pharmacists. Specifically, officials from that state board said that while there is value in DEA enforcement actions such as preventing harmful drugs from being diverted to illegal sales, DEA enforcement actions have created fear among some pharmacists, causing them to be overly cautious when dispensing prescription drugs (e.g., by denying a prescription). Regarding the different interpretation of laws and regulations, the state board officials explained that there was inconsistent interpretation of laws and regulations among DEA field offices, which caused confusion among the board and pharmacists. The board officials said that they contacted DEA for clarification, but this has not resolved the issue.

Many National Associations Interact with DEA, Mostly through Meetings, and While More than Half Were Satisfied Some want Improved Communication

Of the 26 national associations we interviewed, 24 reported interacting with DEA most commonly through hosting or participating in meetings, providing input and comments on regulations, and supporting federal drug disposal efforts to help reduce prescription drug abuse and diversion. While some national associations did not comment directly on their satisfaction with how they interact with DEA, more than half of those that did indicated that they were generally satisfied with those interactions, though others wanted better communication with the agency.

Methods of Interaction with DEA

Of the 24 national associations that interacted with DEA, many reported that they participate in meetings with DEA to obtain and share information related to prescription drug abuse and diversion.[39] Specifically, more than half (15 of 24) of the national associations that interacted with DEA reported that they have hosted meetings in which DEA was invited to be a speaker or participated in meetings where DEA was present. For example, officials from six national associations reported that they invited DEA to their meetings to discuss issues such as changes in regulations or trend data on prescription drug abuse. National associations also interact with DEA as part of larger, national meetings. For example, officials from four national associations reported interacting with DEA by attending the same meetings such as the National Prescription Drug Abuse Summit and Pain Care Forum, where DEA was a presenter. They reported that during these meetings DEA officials discussed such things as best practices for reducing prescription drug abuse and diversion, legitimate prescribing, and patient access to legitimate drugs.

National associations also reported that they have interacted with DEA by providing input or comments on proposed regulations. For example, officials from six national associations we interviewed reported interacting with DEA by providing comments or feedback on DEA's proposed drug disposal rule.[40] Additionally, officials from half of the national associations (12 of 24) we interviewed reported supporting or participating in DEA's prescription drug take-back events. According to officials from four of these national associations, they helped promote the take-back events by publicizing the events on their website for their members and two associations arranged for the collection of unwanted medication from the public.

Satisfaction with DEA Interactions

While some national associations (7 of 24) did not comment on whether they were satisfied with how they interact with DEA, most of those that did indicated that they were generally satisfied with those interactions. Specifically, of the 17 national associations that commented about their satisfaction with their interactions with DEA, 10 indicated that they were generally satisfied, while 7 indicated that they were generally dissatisfied.

Of the national associations that indicated they were generally satisfied, some noted that the information shared by DEA officials during meetings, particularly about trends in prescription drug abuse and diversion, has been helpful, as were DEA's prescription drug take-back events. According to officials from three national associations we interviewed, the trend information they receive from DEA has been helpful in understanding what is happening in different regions related to prescription drug abuse and diversion. Regarding DEA's prescription drug take-back events, officials from a national association reported that the take-back events help to reduce the number of drugs in people's medicine cabinets, which may reduce potential misuse or abuse. One national association that indicated it was generally satisfied with its interactions with DEA also said that it would like to have more communication from DEA. For example, an official from this national association reported that it would be helpful if DEA would provide some type of communication and information that could serve as a checklist of things the association and its members should be aware of, such as tips and trends related to transporting pharmaceuticals.

Among the concerns cited by the seven national associations that were generally dissatisfied with their DEA interactions was insufficient communication and collaboration from DEA. For example, officials from five national associations reported that as prescription drug abuse has increased, DEA has been less collaborative, and officials from two associations noted that DEA refused to meet with them to clarify issues related to their members' CSA responsibilities. DEA officials told us that they did not believe the agency had turned down any requests from associations that wanted to meet, though they acknowledged they were aware that one national association in particular has not been satisfied with DEA and has said that DEA has cut off communications. DEA officials said that the agency communicates with the registrants that this particular association represents, and these registrants should contact DEA directly about any questions related to their roles and responsibilities. Nonetheless, because 4 of the 7 dissatisfied associations indicated that the additional communication they want to have with DEA relates to the CSA roles and responsibilities of their members, improved communication with and guidance for registrants may address some of these associations' concerns.

Many Stakeholders Believe DEA Enforcement Actions have Helped Decrease Prescription Drug Abuse and Diversion, but may also have Limited Legitimate Access

Many of the DEA registrants we surveyed and other stakeholders we interviewed reported that they believe DEA enforcement actions have helped decrease prescription drug abuse and diversion. Nonetheless, over half of DEA registrants reported changing certain business practices as a result of DEA enforcement actions or the business climate these actions may have created, and many of these registrants reported that these changes have limited access to prescription drugs for patients with legitimate medical needs.

"We have been contacted [by DEA] when an investigation has occurred, which alerts us to monitor suspicious orders. This has been helpful as it promptly addresses potential diversion."

Source: GAO distributor survey. | GAO-15-471

Many Stakeholders Believe DEA Enforcement Actions have Helped Decrease Abuse and Diversion, Although Some are Uncertain about Effects

While the majority of DEA registrants have not had DEA enforcement actions taken against them, we estimate that between 31 and 38 percent of registrants that we surveyed, depending on the registrant group, believe DEA enforcement actions have been very or moderately helpful in decreasing abuse and diversion. However, 53 percent of chain pharmacy corporate offices (17 of 32) believe DEA enforcement actions were slightly or not at all helpful and other registrants reported not knowing whether DEA's efforts had an effect, such as practitioner registrants where we estimate that 47 percent don't know the effect of enforcement actions. (See table 6.)

Of the national associations and state agencies we interviewed that offered a perspective on this issue, most (13 of 17) reported that DEA enforcement actions have helped to decrease abuse and diversion of prescription drugs. For example, an official from a state law enforcement agency said that DEA's enforcement efforts had been very helpful in that state, particularly as DEA provided the state with additional resources and worked with local law enforcement. In addition, an official from a national association said that the association has heard from its members how helpful DEA has been in working with some of the statewide and local task forces on diversion-related investigations. An official from another national association said that DEA's enforcement actions have caused some companies to make changes to their corporate practices that have a positive effect on decreasing abuse and diversion. While several of the national associations and state agencies we interviewed said that DEA enforcement actions may be reducing prescription drug abuse and diversion, some are concerned about a resulting substitution of other illegal drug use. For example, officials from one state law enforcement agency said that they are seeing evidence of the reemergence of heroin usage as the availability of prescription drugs has gone down and their cost has gone up.

In addition to obtaining stakeholders' perspectives on how DEA enforcement actions have affected abuse and diversion of prescription drugs, we reviewed data on DEA enforcement actions and investigations from fiscal year 2009 through fiscal year 2013 to identify any trends in DEA activities.[41] Our analyses showed that certain types of administrative enforcement actions—administrative enforcement hearings, letters of admonition, and memoranda of agreement—increased across all registrants during this time period while other administrative enforcement actions—orders to show cause and immediate suspension orders— decreased. Scheduled regulatory investigations also increased during this time period for diversion-related cases, particularly for pharmacy and practitioner registrants. (See app. III for data on DEA enforcement actions and investigations.) Officials from DEA's Office of Diversion Control told us that DEA shifted its work plan in 2009 to put more emphasis on regulatory investigations with the goal of bringing registrants into compliance with the CSA. The officials said the increase in DEA's scheduled regulatory investigations during this period may have helped identify areas in which registrants needed to improve and make changes to be in compliance with their responsibilities under the CSA. They also said that the increase in letters of admonition explains why there was not an increase of orders to show cause or immediate suspension orders, which are more severe penalties. Officials said that DEA considers letters of admonition as a way to help registrants comply with CSA requirements, and if registrants comply, this may help reduce diversion. The officials added that this increase shows that DEA's enforcement efforts are being resolved cooperatively with its registrants, and that as a result DEA has less need to impose harsher penalties on its registrants. However, data are not available to show any direct link between DEA enforcement actions or investigations and decreases in abuse and diversion. In a previous report, we recommended that DEA enhance its performance measures to better track and report on the results its enforcement actions had on reducing diversion of prescription drugs.[42] In its response, DEA stated that it is impossible to measure the lack of diversion, and that enforcement actions help to prevent future diversion, among other things.

Table 6. Registrant Perspectives on the Helpfulness of Drug Enforcement Administration (DEA) Enforcement Actions in Decreasing Abuse and Diversion of Prescription Drugs

Type of respondent	Very or moderately helpful	Slightly or not at all helpful	Don't know
Distributors	35%	31%	34%
Individual pharmacies	36%	28%	36%
Chain pharmacy corporate offices[a]	31% (10)	53% (17)	16% (5)
Practitioners	38%	15%	47%

Source: GAO surveys of DEA registrants. | GAO-15-471

Notes: Between July 2014 and October 2014, we surveyed generalizable random samples of DEA- registered distributors, individual pharmacies, and practitioners, and we surveyed all of the corporate offices of the 38 chain pharmacies we identified using a DEA database. Registrants were asked variations of the following question specific to their registrant type, "From your perspective, how helpful, if at all, have DEA enforcement actions against [DEA registrants] been to efforts to decrease abuse and diversion of prescription drugs?" Percentage estimates for distributors, individual pharmacies, and practitioners are subject to margins of error of no more than ±10 percentage points. Percentages may not add to 100 percent because of rounding.

[a] Responses are from the 32 chain pharmacy corporate offices that responded to our survey. We report both percentages and numbers (in parentheses) for the chain pharmacy corporate office responses because of the small population size.

> "I appreciate pharmacists calling me to verify that I did actually write the prescription--in some cases it is because it was one we could fax and the office it was sent from is unclear. In one case, it was a forged prescription."
>
> Source: GAO practitioner survey. | GAO-15-471

Many Registrants Have Changed Certain Business Practices as a Result of DEA Enforcement Actions and Reported these Changes have Limited Legitimate Access

On the basis of our generalizable surveys, we found that over half of registrants have made changes to certain business practices that they attribute in part to either DEA enforcement actions or the business climate these actions may have created.[43] For example, we estimate that 71 percent of individual pharmacies increased the number of contacts made to prescriber's offices to verify legitimate medical need for prescriptions, and 75 percent of these pharmacies attributed this change to a great or moderate extent to DEA enforcement actions or the business climate those actions have created. (See app. II, tables 23 through 26 for complete data for all four registrant types.)

Some business practice changes may help reduce prescription drug abuse and diversion. For example, in their open-ended responses, several practitioners said that they appreciated getting phone calls from pharmacies verifying the legitimacy of prescriptions because it helped make the practitioner more aware of potential abuse. However, many registrants reported that some of these changes had limited access to prescription drugs for patients with legitimate medical needs. (See table 7 below, and app. II, tables 27 through 30 for additional data.) For example, we estimate that over half of distributors placed stricter thresholds, or limits, on the quantities of controlled substances that their customers (e.g., pharmacies and practitioners) could order, and that most of these distributors were influenced to a great or moderate extent by DEA's enforcement actions. Regarding specific enforcement actions that DEA has taken, in 2011, three distributors agreed to pay fines totaling more than $58 million and, in 2013, two distributors agreed to pay fines totaling more than $80 million, which some registrants and one national association suggested could be influencing distributors' decisions to place thresholds on orders. (See app. III for additional data on civil fines.) Many individual pharmacies and chain pharmacy corporate offices reported that these stricter thresholds have limited, to a great or moderate extent, their ability to supply drugs to those with a legitimate need. (See table 7.)

"As other chains have pushed controlled substance prescriptions out of their stores, many of which are legitimate, we have placed a burden on our current patients when we run up against our thresholds from the [distributor]."

Source: GAO chain pharmacy corporate office survey. | GAO-15-471

In their open-ended responses to our survey, some registrants expanded upon how DEA enforcement actions have affected their business practices, and subsequently affected patient access. A chain pharmacy corporate office reported that pharmacists are afraid of being the target of DEA enforcement actions even if they fill a prescription in good faith and with good judgment. Instead of erring on the side of a patient when considering filling a prescription, the chain pharmacy corporate office said that pharmacists are taking actions to try to protect their DEA registration that come at the expense of the patient. For example, one individual pharmacy reported that it turned away patients without taking steps to verify whether a controlled substance prescription was legitimate because the pharmacy could not serve new controlled substance patients without risking being cut off by its distributor. This pharmacy said that DEA has clearly stated that it is not calling for distributor cutoffs (i.e., thresholds), but their distributors have communicated that these changes are made because of fear of DEA enforcement actions, which has led many pharmacies to refuse to fill legitimate prescriptions. A distributor reported it refuses to distribute large volumes of controlled substances to prescribers or pharmacies that specialize in pain management, even if it has no evidence that the prescribers or pharmacies are engaged in diversion. This distributor said that DEA has stated that the agency would hold distributors accountable for diversion that occurs at the prescriber and pharmacy level. Therefore, according to this distributor, supplying a large volume of controlled substances to customers with a pain management practice creates too great a risk of being the target of a DEA enforcement action for them to continue to service such requests. Further, several individual pharmacies expressed concern in their open- ended responses that certain business practices, such as distributors placing thresholds on their orders for controlled substances, have affected their ability to care for patients by limiting access to these drugs.

"As a small family-owned company we can ill afford the negative press as well as the fines [resulting from a DEA enforcement action]. We are very serious about [prescription drug abuse and diversion] so we take things to the extreme to the point where we have received complaints from providers for turning away legitimate patients. We don't have the resources available like the major corporations so we take the most conservative approach."

Source: GAO chain pharmacy corporate office survey. | GAO-15-471

A few national associations also spoke of indirect effects resulting from the business climate that enforcement actions have created, which could ultimately result in limiting access for legitimate needs. For example, one national association said that following a large DEA fine against one distributor, and in the absence of clear DEA guidance, distributors became concerned about how to determine that an order is suspicious. Therefore, distributors elected to arbitrarily set thresholds for the amount of controlled substances pharmacies could order. In addition, an official from another national association said that prescribers find it difficult to address the questions from pharmacists about patients' need for certain prescription medication and this affects the prescriber's time in providing care to the patients and could affect patient access to certain medication.

Table 7. Examples of Business Practice Changes Taken by Drug Enforcement Administration (DEA) Registrants and the Potential Effect These Actions Could Have on Legitimate Access

	Distributors	**Chain pharmacy corporate offices**[a]	**Individual pharmacies**	**Practitioners**
Action taken by registrants	Placed stricter thresholds on orders	Increased the number of contacts made to prescriber's offices to verify the legitimacy of prescriptions	Increased the number of delays in filling prescriptions to check for legitimate medical need	Increased the number ofquestions asked to patients before prescribing, dispensing, or administering certain controlled substances
Percentage of registrants that took the action	57%	97% (31)	58%	51%
Of those registrants that took the action, percentage that greatly/moderately attributed action to DEA actions	84%	90% (28)	69%	65%
Extent to which other registrants reported that the action taken limited access to prescription drugs for legitimate medical needs	52 out of 84 individual pharmacies and 18 of 29 chain pharmacy corporate offices said that, to a great or moderate extent, the stricter thresholds limited their ability to supply drugs to those with a legitimate need	17 out of 41 practitioners said that, to a great or moderate extent, the increased number of calls to prescriber's offices limited their ability to supply drugs to those with a legitimate need	15 out of 38 practitioners said that, to a great or moderate extent, the increased number of delays in filling prescriptions limited their ability to supply drugs to those with a legitimate need	n/a[b]

Source: GAO surveys of DEA registrants. | GAO-15-471

Notes: Between July 2014 and October 2014, we surveyed generalizable random samples of DEA- registered distributors, individual pharmacies, and practitioners, and we surveyed all of the corporate offices of the 38 chain pharmacies we identified using a DEA database. Registrants were asked variations of the following questions specific to their registrant type, "[Have you] made any of the following changes related to controlled substances since Jan. 1, 2012? If so, to what extent was that change influenced by DEA enforcement actions against registrants or as a result of the business climate those actions may have created?" and "[Have you] experienced any of the following actions taken by [manufacturer, distributor, pharmacy] since Jan. 1, 2012?, If so, in general, to what extent has that action limited your ability to [prescribe, dispense, or otherwise handle] controlled substances?' Percentage estimates for distributors, individual pharmacies, and practitioners are subject to margins of error of no more than ±10 percentage points. Percentage estimates with margins of error greater than 10 percentage points were reported as numbers instead of percentages in the table.

[a] Responses are from the 32 chain pharmacy corporate offices that responded to our survey. We report both percentages and numbers (in parentheses) for the chain pharmacy corporate office responses because of the small population size.

[b] No other registrants were asked to comment on this business practice change as this action was taken by practitioners with respect to patients, not other registrants.

Of the national associations and state agencies we interviewed that offered a perspective on the potential for limited access, more than half (19 of 28) expressed concern that DEA's enforcement actions have limited access to these drugs for legitimate medical needs. For example, officials from one state agency said that DEA has taken actions against pharmacists in that state that has caused concerns among some pharmacists resulting in instances where legitimate patients with a legitimate prescription are being denied access to prescription drugs.

However, DEA officials in the four DEA field office divisions we spoke with said that they generally did not think that their enforcement actions have had a negative effect on access, and headquarters officials from DEA's Office of Diversion Control indicated that they did not believe their enforcement actions had any bearing on access issues. DEA field office officials said that they have rarely heard about any access concerns, although neither DEA field office nor headquarters officials indicated that they have taken steps to obtain any information about the extent of access issues. DEA headquarters officials said that they could not tell a distributor that a pharmacy is ordering too many controlled substances; there are no federal quotas on these orders. Additionally, DEA headquarters officials said that if access is limited the patient should contact his or her state pharmacy association and explain the situation and that the state pharmacy board could intervene. DEA headquarters officials also told us that if a pharmacy is unable to fill a prescription because distributor thresholds have limited the amount of drugs the pharmacy has available to fill prescriptions, that pharmacy should help the patients find another pharmacy where they can get the medications, as they should in any case in which the pharmacy could not fill a prescription. However, while DEA's recommendation may be valid for some patients, it does not take into account that certain patients could experience hardships in trying to find another pharmacy to get their prescription filled. For example, patients living in rural areas may have a limited number of pharmacies nearby, and some patients, such as those with cancer, may be too ill to travel to different pharmacies for their medications.

As previously noted, internal control standards for federal agencies state that management should ensure there are adequate means of communicating with stakeholders that may have a significant impact on the agency achieving its goals.[44] If access issues to prescription drugs for patients with legitimate medical needs are resulting from DEA registrants being unclear about their roles and responsibilities under the CSA, and registrants have not proactively raised concerns about access issues directly with DEA, more regular communication with its registrants, as previously discussed, could provide the agency with more opportunities to obtain registrants' input regarding concerns about access issues. Further, more regular communication between DEA and its registrants, including clearer guidance, could help to mitigate registrants' fears of taking actions that would make them targets of DEA enforcement actions and investigations, and help registrants make business decisions that balance ensuring that patients have access to needed medications with controlling abuse and diversion.

CONCLUSIONS

The magnitude of the prescription drug abuse problem, including high rates of overdose deaths, requires a response from all levels of government, industry, and other stakeholders. And while many federal agencies have important responsibilities in addressing prescription drug abuse and diversion, DEA plays a key role because it administers and enforces the CSA, and in doing so interacts with a wide range of nonfederal entities that are stakeholders in the prescription drug supply chain. DEA faces a significant challenge in simultaneously ensuring the availability of controlled substances for legitimate use while limiting their availability for diversion and abuse. Therefore, adequate DEA communication with and guidance for its registrants are essential to help ensure that registrants take actions that prevent abuse and diversion but do not unnecessarily diminish patients' access to controlled substances for legitimate use because of their uncertainty about how to appropriately meet their CSA roles and responsibilities.

While many of the registrants, state government agencies, and national associations that have interacted with DEA were generally satisfied with these interactions, some of these stakeholders said they needed improved communication and guidance regarding registrants' roles and responsibilities for preventing abuse and diversion under the CSA. More DEA communication with registrants could help improve their awareness of various DEA resources, as well as help DEA better understand registrants' information needs, such as their need for improved guidance. While providing additional guidance to registrants—particularly distributors and pharmacies—about their CSA roles and responsibilities cannot ensure that registrants are meeting them, by doing so DEA will have a greater assurance that registrants understand their CSA responsibilities. Additionally, DEA has stated that its goal is bringing registrants into compliance rather than taking enforcement actions, and DEA can move closer towards this goal by improving its communication and information sharing with registrants, consistent with federal internal controls standards.

RECOMMENDATIONS FOR EXECUTIVE ACTION

In order to strengthen DEA's communication with and guidance for registrants and associations representing registrants, as well as supporting the Office of Diversion Control's mission of preventing diversion while ensuring an adequate and uninterrupted supply of controlled substances for legitimate medical needs, we recommend that the Deputy Assistant Administrator for the Office of Diversion Control take the following three actions:

- Identify and implement means of cost-effective, regular communication with distributor, pharmacy, and practitioner registrants, such as through listservs or web-based training.
- Solicit input from distributors, or associations representing distributors, and develop additional guidance for distributors regarding their roles and responsibilities for suspicious orders monitoring and reporting.
- Solicit input from pharmacists, or associations representing pharmacies and pharmacists, about updates and additions needed to existing guidance for pharmacists, and revise or issue guidance accordingly.

AGENCY COMMENTS AND OUR EVALUATION

We provided a draft copy of this report to the Department of Justice for its review and DEA's Office of Diversion Control provided written comments. In its comments, DEA stated that it describes the actions that it plans to take to implement our three recommendations. However, we identified additional actions DEA should take to fully implement our recommendations.

In addition to providing comments on the recommendations, DEA also commented on other aspects of our draft report, including some of the results and conclusions from our surveys, and referred to some survey results as anecdotal data. Because our surveys were designed and conducted to produce reliable and generalizable estimates, we are confident that our survey results accurately represent the perspectives of registrants about their interactions with DEA and their concerns about their roles and responsibilities under the CSA. We are also confident that the conclusions we drew from the survey results were reasonable and appropriate.

Regarding our first recommendation to identify and implement means of cost-effective, regular communication with distributor, pharmacy, and practitioner registrants, DEA agreed that communication from DEA to the registrant population is necessary and vital. The agency stated that it is in the planning stages of developing web-based training modules for its registrant population, to include training for pharmacists on their corresponding responsibilities and potential training for manufacturers and distributors to include ARCOS reporting and how to request a quota. While DEA did not specifically mention developing training for distributors on suspicious orders monitoring in its comments, our survey results suggest that this type of training for distributors would also be helpful. DEA also stated that it is considering implementing a listserv to disseminate information on various topics to its registrants, including information on cases involving diversion of controlled substances, and will continue to explore other means of cost-effective communication with its registrants. Additionally, while DEA agreed that communication with its registrants is necessary and vital, it also suggested that registrants that are not in frequent communication with the agency do not deem such communication to be necessary and noted that its registrant community has not broached the subject of additional guidance or communication. However, our survey data show that registrants are not fully aware of DEA conferences and resources and want additional guidance from, and communication with, the agency. Therefore, we continue to believe that it is DEA's responsibility to reach out to its registrants, and believe that doing so will help DEA better understand registrants' information needs.

DEA raised concerns about our second recommendation to solicit input from distributors, or associations representing distributors, and develop additional guidance for distributors regarding their roles and responsibilities for suspicious orders monitoring and reporting. DEA stated that short of providing arbitrary thresholds to distributors, it cannot provide more specific suspicious orders guidance because the variables that indicate a suspicious order differ among distributors and their customers. Instead, DEA highlighted regulations that require distributors to design and operate systems to disclose suspicious orders. However, according to DEA's Customer Service Plan for Registrants, DEA is responsible for developing guidance for registrants regarding the CSA and its regulations, and the agency was able to create such guidance for pharmacy and practitioner registrants. DEA also noted that it has steadily increased the frequency of compliance inspections of distributors in recent years. DEA stated that this has enabled the agency to take a more proactive approach in educating its registrants and ensuring that registrants understand and comply with the CSA and its implementing regulations. While we agree that inspections provide registrants with an opportunity for communication with DEA and may provide specific information related to compliance with the CSA, we do not believe that formal inspections provide registrants with a neutral educational setting in which to obtain a better understanding of their CSA roles and responsibilities. DEA also provided examples of how the agency has provided additional information related to suspicious orders monitoring to distributor registrants who participate in its Distributor Initiative briefings and its distributor conferences. Therefore, we continue to believe that DEA could provide additional written guidance for distributors that could be more widely accessible to all distributor registrants. DEA did not comment on whether it plans to solicit input from distributors, or associations representing distributors, on developing additional distributor guidance, and we continue to believe that obtaining input from these parties would help DEA better understand distributors' needs related to their CSA roles and responsibilities.

With regard to our third recommendation to solicit input from pharmacists, or associations representing pharmacies and pharmacists, about updates and additions needed to existing guidance for pharmacists, and revise or issue guidance accordingly, DEA described actions it would take to partially address the recommendation. Specifically, DEA stated that it would work to update the Pharmacist's Manual to reflect two subject matter area changes made since the manual was last updated in 2010— (1) the rescheduling of hydrocodone from schedule III to schedule II and (2) the new rules on disposal of controlled substances. However, DEA did not comment about providing any additional guidance to pharmacists related to their roles and responsibilities in preventing abuse and diversion under the CSA. Because our survey results showed that this was a primary area of concern for individual pharmacies and chain pharmacy corporate offices, we believe any updates to the Pharmacist's Manual should also include additional information specific to pharmacists' corresponding responsibilities under the CSA. DEA also did not comment on whether it plans to solicit input from pharmacists, or associations representing pharmacies and pharmacists, on updating and revising guidance for pharmacists; however, we continue to believe such input would be beneficial for DEA to better understand its pharmacy registrants' needs and how best to address them.

Linda T. Kohn
Director, Health Care

George A. Scott
Managing Director, Homeland Security and Justice

APPENDIX I: OBJECTIVES, SCOPE, AND METHODOLOGY

This report examines (1) how and to what extent selected registrants interact with the Drug Enforcement Administration (DEA) related to their responsibilities for preventing prescription drug abuse and diversion under the Controlled Substances Act (CSA), and registrants' perspectives on those interactions, (2) how selected state agencies and national associations interact with DEA related to reducing prescription drug abuse and diversion, and their perspectives on those interactions, and (3) stakeholders' perspectives about how DEA enforcement actions have affected abuse and diversion of prescription drugs and access to those drugs for legitimate medical needs.[45]

To address our first and third objectives, we administered four web-based nationally representative surveys to the following three types of DEA registrants: drug distributors, pharmacies, and practitioners. To further address all three objectives we interviewed government officials from 16 agencies in four states (California, Florida, Kentucky, and New York), officials at 26 national associations and nonprofit organizations (referred to as "national associations" throughout this report), and officials at both DEA headquarters and selected field offices. Finally, to help address our third objective, we reviewed data on DEA's enforcement actions from fiscal year 2009 through fiscal year 2013 that were taken against DEA registrants in the three categories that we included in our surveys (distributors, pharmacies, and practitioners) to identify any trends in DEA's enforcement actions over a recent time period.

2014 Surveys of Distributors, Individual Pharmacies, Chain Pharmacy Corporate Offices, and Practitioners

To address the first and third objectives, we surveyed samples of practitioners, distributors, and pharmacies that were registered with the DEA to prescribe, administer, or handle controlled substances about their interactions with DEA and perspectives on DEA enforcement. The survey was designed to collect detailed reports from registrants and make generalizable estimates of the nature and extent of their interaction with DEA programs and staff related to registrant responsibilities under the CSA. The survey was also designed to measure registrant perceptions of the impact of DEA enforcement actions on: their own business practices, or the business climate in which they operate, as well as their perspectives on whether enforcement actions have had an effect on reducing abuse and diversion or on limiting patients' access to prescription drugs for legitimate medical needs.

Of the approximately 1.5 million DEA registrants as of January 2014, the target populations for our survey were restricted to distributors, pharmacies, and practitioners in specific business activity categories. We selected these categories of registrants because they are the primary DEA registrants in the prescription drug supply chain and are more likely to be the focus of DEA enforcement actions than other categories of registrants such as researchers or drug importers. Our target populations were also restricted to those with an active registration status; eligible to distribute, dispense, administer, or prescribe either Schedule II or III drugs; and located in the continental United States. We used DEA's CSA Master File, as of January 13, 2014, to define the target populations, and to create the listings from which we drew our survey samples. Our target populations also excluded additional identifiable registrants outside the scope of our review such as federal government registrants, veterinarians or veterinary-oriented businesses, and research-oriented academic registrants.[46]

Distributors in our target population were restricted to those registrants with the DEA business activity code F and subcode 0. Pharmacies were restricted to those with activity code A and subcodes 0 ("Retail Pharmacies"), 1 ("Central Fill Pharmacies"—later excluded from being included in the survey sample if not part of a chain pharmacy corporation), or 3 ("Chain Pharmacies"). Practitioners in our target population were restricted to those with activity codes and subcodes listed in table 8.

Table 8. Drug Enforcement Administration (DEA) Registrant Practitioners Included in the GAO Survey Target Population

DEA business activity code	DEA business activity subcode	Definition
C	0	Practitioner
C	1	Practitioner-DW/30 (Drug Addiction Treatment Act-waived (DW) medical doctor or doctor of osteopathic medicine authorized to treat up to 30 addicted patients)
C	4	Practitioner-DW/100 (Drug Addiction Treatment Act-waived (DW) medical doctor or doctor of osteopathic medicine authorized to treat up to 100 addicted patients)
M	1	Mid-level practitioner (MLP) – Ambulance service
M	3	MLP – Doctor of Oriental Medicine
M	6	MLP – Homeopathic physician
M	7	MLP – Medical Psychologist
M	8	MLP – Naturopathic Physician
M	9	MLP – Nursing Home
M	A	MLP – Nurse Practitioner
M	B	MLP - Optometrist
M	C	MLP – Physician Assistant
M	D	MLP – Registered Pharmacist

Source: DEA. | GAO-15-471

The total number of registrants in the DEA CSA Master File database that we received, and the total number of registrants initially designated as eligible for the target populations, prior to sampling, are listed in table 9.

The pharmacy target population was subdivided into two populations to be surveyed: "individual pharmacies"—stores that were independently owned, or part of a corporation with less than 50 total locations—and "chain pharmacy corporate offices" that had 50 or more registered locations.[47] Processing the CSA Master File database with those specifications and performing additional manual screening resulted in a final individual pharmacy survey population of 32,207, and a survey population of 38 chain pharmacy corporate offices.[48] Manual screening of the population listings during sampling also resulted in excluding practitioner registrants who were primarily in academic, federal government, or veterinary practice, and those practitioners or distributors that were no longer prescribing, administering, storing or handling controlled substances. The resulting four target populations were: distributors, individual pharmacies, chain pharmacy corporate offices, and practitioners.

Table 9. Numbers of Drug Enforcement Administration (DEA) Registrants as of January 2014 and Numbers of Registrants Included in GAO Survey Target Population

DEA registrant type	DEA registrant totals	GAO target population totals
Distributors	965[a]	787
Pharmacies	69,676	68,880[b]
Practitioners	1,415,856[c]	1,344,567
Other DEA registrants[d]	30,126	Not included
Total	**1,516,623**	**1,414,234**

Source: DEA and GAO analysis of DEA's Controlled Substances Act Master File database. | GAO-15-471

[a] Chempak Distributors (activity subcode 1) were included in the DEA total but excluded from the target population.

[b] Registrants represent individual business locations. Pharmacies were later aggregated into either chain pharmacy corporate offices or individual pharmacies.

[c] Practitioners included in the DEA total but excluded from the target population include military, Department of Defense contractor, or other federal government registrants, veterinarians, and euthanasia technicians.

[d] Other DEA registrant types include manufacturers, hospitals and clinics, importers/exporters of controlled substances, narcotic treatment programs, and researchers who use controlled substances or medications in their research or analyses. These registrants were excluded from the target populations.

From the four target population lists, we drew simple random samples of sufficient sizes (see table 11) to account for reductions due to nonresponse, additional ineligibility, and the variability introduced by sampling, to yield percentage estimates from survey questions generalizable to each of the four populations with confidence intervals (sampling error, or the margin of error) no wider than ±10 percentage points at the 95 percent level of confidence. This planned level of precision applied only to questions to be asked of the entire sample; questions asked of only a subset of the sample would produce estimates with wider confidence intervals.

We designed and tested four questionnaires, asking parallel questions tailored to each of the four populations. We consulted with subject matter experts in professional trade associations and survey methodologists, and reviewed past surveys of these populations and subjects. We also conducted cognitive interview pretests of draft versions of the questionnaires with registrants from each population (three practitioners, two distributors, one individual pharmacy, and two chain pharmacy corporate offices), and obtained a quality review by a separate GAO survey methodologist. Based on these developmental and evaluation activities, we made changes to the four draft questionnaires before administering them.

Each questionnaire focused on four primary topic areas, made up of questions appropriate for the population:

1. awareness, use, and rating of DEA guidance, resources, and tools for understanding registrant responsibilities related to the CSA;
2. nature, extent, and ratings of interactions with DEA headquarters or field staff related to CSA responsibilities through DEA conferences, initiatives, training, and other communication;
3. interaction with other federal agencies; and
4. impact of DEA enforcement actions on registrant business practices, including opinions on the effect of DEA enforcement actions on drug abuse and diversion and legitimate access to controlled substances.

Individual pharmacies were asked to respond to the survey on behalf of their single pharmacy location that was selected in our sample, regardless of its ownership status. Chain pharmacy corporate offices were asked to respond to the survey on behalf of all of their registered pharmacy locations.

The surveys were administered using a mixed-mode approach. Web questionnaire format was the primary mode, and each of the surveys used an initial data collection attempt using emailed username, password, and link to a questionnaire website. When email addresses were not available, or found to be nonworking, mail or phone contacts were made to obtain emails, to direct registrants to the website, or, as a secondary mode of response for practitioners and individual pharmacies, to fax or mail paper versions of the questionnaires. For practitioners, of the 208 usable responses, 47 were received in paper format. For individual pharmacies, of the 170 usable responses, 20 were received in paper format.

A variety of contacts were made with each sample during survey fieldwork. For practitioners and individual pharmacies, an advance letter was mailed to all sampled registrants in late June and early July of 2014. Telephone contacts were made before and during fieldwork to obtain missing or incorrect contact information, encourage response, and determine final outcomes such as ineligibility or refusal. Paper questionnaires were mailed to nonresponding practitioner and individual pharmacy registrants; letters with web survey login information were mailed to distributors during the follow-up period. GAO staff made direct contacts with chain pharmacy corporate offices to manage survey administration. The key steps and dates of data collection are described in table 10.

Table 10. Key Survey Fieldwork Dates for GAO Survey of Drug Enforcement Administration Registrants

	Practitioners	Distributors	Individual pharmacies	Chain pharmacy corporate offices
Data collection began (emails or paper questionnaires sent)	7/29/14	8/25/14	8/14/14	8/14/14
Email, mail, phone follow-up contacts	8/12/14 – 8/26/14	9/9/14 – 9/24/14	8/25/14 – 9/26/14	9/4/14 – 10/13/14
Final email notification of survey closing	9/30/14	10/7/14	10/9/14	n/a
Data collection ended (no additional responses accepted)	10/2/14	10/29/14	10/15/14	10/13/14

Source: GAO. | GAO-15-471

Table 11. GAO Survey Samples and Fieldwork Outcomes

	Practitioners	Distributors	Individual pharmacies	Chain pharmacy corporate offices
Initial sample screened for eligibility	426	241	345	38
Ineligibles screened from initial sample	26	41	41	0
Final sample surveyed	400	200	304	38
Ineligibles found in survey	9	1	16	0
Nonrespondents known to be eligible	41	17	28	6
Nonrespondents of unknown eligibility	142	11	90	0
Usable responses	208	171	170	32
Proportion of nonrespondents of unknown eligibility estimated to be eligible[a]	90%	90%	82%	n/a
Response rate[b]	55%	86%	63%	84%

Source: GAO. | GAO-15-471

[a] The rate of eligibility among nonrespondents of unknown eligibility was assumed to be the same as the rate found across the initially screened and surveyed sample cases where it was determined. Some types of ineligibles found during initial sample screening, such as registrants with addresses outside of the United States, were easily identifiable and likely to have been completely removed before the survey. Because additional ineligibles of this type were not likely to be found among those of unknown eligibility, those ineligibles were not included in the calculation of the eligibility rate. For practitioners, 19 of the 26 initially screened ineligibles were considered indicative of ineligibles that could occur among survey nonrespondents, and so were included in the calculation of the eligibility rate. For distributors, 19 of the 41 ineligibles were included. For individual pharmacies, 27 of 41 ineligibles were included. For chain corporate pharmacy offices, there were no nonrespondents of unknown eligibility.

[b] American Association for Public Opinion Research response rate formula RR3 was used for practitioners, distributors, and individual pharmacies. RR1 was used for chain pharmacy corporate offices. See American Association for Public Opinion Research, *Standard Definitions – Final Dispositions of Case Codes and Outcome Rates for Surveys*, accessed April 23, 2015, http://www.aapor.org/AAPORKentico/Communications/AAPOR-Journals/Standard-Definitions.aspx.

After the survey fieldwork period closed, the outcomes of the original samples drawn were tallied. (See table 11.)

Each questionnaire, except for those sent to chain pharmacy corporate offices, began with a filter question to determine whether the sampled registrant had prescribed, dispensed administered, stored or handled controlled substances in the approximately two years prior to the survey (or, in the case of individual pharmacies, “currently”). This was known with certainty for the chain pharmacy corporate offices, but some of the respondents in the other registrant samples had not performed this activity: 14 percent of practitioners, 11 percent of distributors, and 4 percent of individual pharmacies reported that they had not performed this activity in the last two years, or currently. These respondents were not asked the rest of the survey questions, which were only applicable to the subset of 179 practitioners, 152 distributors, and 162 individual pharmacies that had performed these activities recently.

We statistically adjusted, or weighted, survey results to multiply the contribution of each responding member of the sample, to produce estimates that represented the entire population. Weights greater than one were applied to all but the chain pharmacy corporate office survey results, which were not based on a sample, as that survey included all 38 members of the target population as we defined, each contributing a weight of one.

Because we followed a probability procedure based on random selections, our samples are only three of a large number of samples that we might have drawn. As each sample could have provided different estimates, we express our confidence in the precision of our particular samples' results as 95 percent confidence intervals (e.g., from x to y percent). This is the interval that would contain the actual population value for 95 percent of the samples we could have drawn. As a result, we are 95 percent confident that each of the confidence intervals based on our survey includes the true values in the sample population. Throughout this report, the confidence intervals surrounding our estimates are no more than plus or minus 10 percentage points, unless otherwise noted.

In addition to sampling error, questionnaire surveys are subject to other potential errors: failure to include all eligible members in the listing of the population, measurement errors when administering the questions, nonresponse error from failing to collect information on some or all questions from those sampled, and data processing error. We took steps to limit each type of error. The DEA CSA Master File database we used to create our listings of the populations was assessed as reliable and likely the most comprehensive listing of DEA registrants. Our manual screening and presurvey contacts with the original oversamples mitigated this potential source of error. Our survey design, testing and evaluation steps were intended to reduce measurement error. Because response rates for practitioners and individual pharmacies fell below 80 percent, a level generally accepted as an indicator of potentially increasing risk of bias due to missing data, we performed nonresponse bias analyses to determine whether those not responding would have answered in a fundamentally different way on key questions we asked. Based on the information available to us to compare respondents to nonrespondents, we found no evidence of a difference on a characteristic that might reasonably be expected to determine the propensity or nature of response. Finally, all data processing and analysis programming was verified by a separate data analyst, and sample and response tracking datasets were independently reviewed.

We analyzed survey responses and compared them to federal internal control standards related to information and communication and the standards in DEA's Office of Diversion Control Customer Service Plan for Registrants.[49]

Interviews with Officials in State Government Agencies, National Associations, and DEA

To further address our objectives, we interviewed government officials at 16 agencies in four states (California, Florida, Kentucky, and New York) and officials at 26 national associations to obtain information about interactions with DEA, their perspectives about those interactions, and their views about the effects of DEA enforcement actions on abuse and diversion and access to legitimate prescription medication. We selected these four states based on the following criteria: (1) had varied drug overdose death rates per 100,000 people based on 2010 CDC data, (2) received federal grants for their prescription drug monitoring programs in 2012 and 2013 from the Department of Justice's Bureau of Justice Assistance, and the Department of Health and Human Services' Substance Abuse and Mental Health Services Administration, (3) represented different geographic regions of the country (as represented by DEA domestic field divisions), and (4) were among states that were mentioned by national associations during our interviews as having unique or innovative initiatives to address prescription drug abuse and diversion. In each of the four states, we interviewed officials that represented the state's Controlled Substances Authority, pharmacy board, medical board, law enforcement agency, and the agency that oversees the state's prescription drug monitoring program, for a total of 16 state agencies.[50] The 26 national associations represented patients, practitioners, pharmacies and pharmacists, distributors, state regulatory authorities, state and local law enforcement, and drug manufacturers, among other relevant stakeholder types.[51] Although the perspectives we obtained during the interviews with state agencies and national associations are not generalizable, the interviews provided insights regarding how these types of entities interact with DEA as well as indicating common areas of concern.

We also obtained documents from and interviewed DEA Office of Diversion Control officials who have oversight responsibility for DEA registrants and are engaged in addressing prescription drug abuse and diversion to learn about how DEA interacts with its registrants and other nonfederal stakeholders, and to obtain DEA's perspectives on information we obtained from our survey results and interviews with nonfederal stakeholders.

In addition, we interviewed officials in DEA field offices in each of the four states in our study, such as supervisors overseeing both diversion investigators and special agents, to obtain their views about engaging with state agencies on efforts related to reducing prescription drug abuse and diversion. We interviewed officials in the following four DEA field offices: the Miami Division, the San Francisco Division, the Kentucky District Office, and the New York Division. We compared DEA's responses regarding its interactions with registrants and nonfederal stakeholders to federal internal control standards related to information and communication and the standards in DEA's Office of Diversion Control Customer Service Plan for Registrants.[52]

Review of DEA Investigations and Enforcement Actions Data

To further address our third objective, we reviewed data on DEA investigations and enforcement actions from fiscal year 2009 through fiscal year 2013 that were taken against the DEA registrant categories that we included in our survey. We examined the data to determine if there were any trends over a recent time period. Investigations included regulatory investigations (i.e., scheduled investigations or inspections conducted every 2, 3, or 5 years), complaint investigations, and criminal investigations. Enforcement actions included administrative actions (e.g., formal administrative hearings, letters of admonition to advise registrants of any violations, and orders to show cause to initiate revocation or suspension of a registration), civil actions, where penalties generally include monetary fines, and criminal actions, where penalties generally include incarceration and fines. We determined that the data were sufficiently reliable for purposes of our report.

We conducted this performance audit from August 2013 to June 2015 in accordance with generally accepted government auditing standards. Those standards require that we plan and perform the audit to obtain sufficient, appropriate evidence to provide a reasonable basis for our findings and conclusions based on our audit objectives. We believe that the evidence obtained provides a reasonable basis for our findings and conclusions based on our audit objectives.

APPENDIX II: DRUG ENFORCEMENT ADMINISTRATION (DEA) REGISTRANT SURVEY DATA

Tables 12 through 30 contain selected data from our surveys of DEA registrants. Between July 30, 2014 and October 14, 2014, we surveyed generalizable random samples of distributors, individual pharmacies, and practitioners, and we surveyed all of the corporate offices of the 38 chain pharmacies we identified using a DEA database. Percentages that are cited are weighted to represent the population. Generally, actual numbers of responses are cited when the number of responses for any registrant type in a particular table fell below 100.

Table 12. Number of Distributors and Practitioners Reporting Various Frequencies of Communication with Drug Enforcement Administration (DEA) Headquarters (HQ) and Field Office Staff

	Distributors		Practitioners	
	HQ	**Field office**	**HQ**	**Field office**
Total respondents with any communication	**104**	**120**	**20**	**13**
Not applicable – no communication	40	2	n/a	n/a
At least once a month	9	26	0	0
Less than once a month, but at least once a quarter	9	28	0	0
Less than once a quarter, but at least once a year	14	33	7	1
Less than once a year	20	24	11	8
Other	12	7	2	4

Source: GAO surveys of DEA registrants. | GAO-15-471

Notes: Between July 2014 and October 2014, we surveyed generalizable random samples of DEA-registered distributors and practitioners. Registrants reporting any direct communications with DEA headquarters or field office staff about their roles and responsibilities since Jan. 1, 2012, were then asked variations of the question "Typically, how often do [you/representatives of this facility] communicate with DEA headquarters/field office staff?" Not all registrants that reported communicating with DEA responded regarding the frequency of their communication. An "n/a" indicates that the question or response was not offered to that registrant type.

Table 13. Number of Individual Pharmacies and Chain Pharmacy Corporate Offices Reporting Various Frequencies of Communication with Drug Enforcement Administration (DEA) Headquarters (HQ) and Field Office Staff

	Individual pharmacies		Chain pharmacy corporate offices	
	HQ	**Field office**	**HQ**	**Field office**
Total respondents with any communication	**45**	**39**	**19**	**27**
At least once a day	0	0	0	1
Less than once a day, but at least once a week	0	0	1	1
Less than once a week, but at least once a month	0	0	0	6
Less than once a month, but at least once a quarter	3	0	8	7
Less than once a quarter, but at least once a year	16	15	3	10
Less than once a year	24	23	4	2
Other	2	1	2	0

Source: GAO surveys of DEA registrants. | GAO-15-471

Notes: Between August 2014 and October 2014, we surveyed a generalizable random sample of DEA-registered individual pharmacies, and we surveyed all of the corporate offices of the 38 chain pharmacies we identified using a DEA database. Registrants reporting any communications with headquarters or field office staff about their roles and responsibilities since Jan. 1, 2012, were then asked variations of the question "Typically, how often do [you/representatives of this pharmacy chain] communicate with DEA headquarters/field office staff?" Not all registrants that reported communicating with DEA responded regarding the frequency of their communication.

Table 14. Number of Registrants Reporting Various Methods of Communication with Drug Enforcement Administration (DEA) Headquarters (HQ) and Field Office Staff

	Distributors		Individual pharmacies		Chain pharmacy corporate offices		Practitioners	
	HQ	**Field office**	**HQ**	**Field office**	**HQ**	**Field office**	**HQ**	**Field office**
Total respondents with any communication	**91**	**120**	**45**	**39**	**19**	**27**	**20**	**13**

	Distributors		Individual pharmacies		Chain pharmacy corporate offices		Practitioners	
	HQ	**Field office**	**HQ**	**Field office**	**HQ**	**Field office**	**HQ**	**Field office**
Telephone	32	88	34	27	16	24	8	7
Postal mail	8	26	10	3	6	6	7	4
E-mail	28	80	17	9	9	16	10	1
In person	6	91	6	16	9	12	3	4
Don't know	3	0	0	1	1	2	0	0
Other	12	3	1	2	1	2	2	1

Source: GAO surveys of DEA registrants. | GAO-15-471

Notes: Between July 2014 and October 2014, we surveyed generalizable random samples of DEA-registered distributors, individual pharmacies, and practitioners, and we surveyed all of the corporate offices of the 38 chain pharmacies we identified using a DEA database. Registrants reporting any communication with headquarters or field office staff about their roles and responsibilities since Jan. 1, 2012, were then asked variations of the question "What forms of communication took place?" Registrants that reported communicating with DEA could then provide responses for one or more methods of communication; however, some did not report any methods.

Table 15. Reasons for Not Participating in a Drug Enforcement Administration (DEA) Conference or Initiative – Distributors

	DEA's October 2013 Distributor Conference	**DEA Distributor Initiative briefing**
Distributors not participating	72%	77%
Reason for not participating		
The conference/briefing was attended by corporate office or other company staff	38%	12%
Not aware of the conference/briefings	35%	49%
Was not able to attend	20%	1%
Did not believe it would be helpful	4%	1%
A briefing has not been offered to us by DEA	n/a	33%
Already participated in a briefing prior to Jan. 1, 2012	n/a	4%
A briefing has been scheduled but has not yet taken place	n/a	0
Other	8%	4%
Don't know	6%	6%

Source: GAO survey of distributors. | GAO-15-471

Notes: Between August 2014 and October 2014, we surveyed a generalizable random sample of DEA-registered distributors. A total of 151 distributors answered the questions: "Did representatives of this facility participate in [DEA's October 2013 Distributor Conference held in National Harbor Maryland]/[in a DEA Distributor Initiative briefing since Jan. 1, 2012]?" Distributors not participating were then asked the following questions: "IF NO PARTICIPATION: Which of the following reasons best describe why representatives of this facility did not participate in [DEA's Distributor Conference]/[a DEA Distributor Initiative briefing since Jan. 1, 2012]?" Distributors that reported that they had not participated in the Distributor Conference or a Distributor Initiative briefing could then provide responses for one or more reasons for not participating. Percentage estimates for distributors are subject to margins of error of no more than ±10 percentage points. Percentages may not add to 100 percent because of rounding. An "n/a" indicates that the response choice was not relevant for that question.

Table 16. Number of Individual Pharmacies and Chain Pharmacy Corporate Offices Reporting Various Reasons for Not Participating in a Drug Enforcement Administration (DEA) Pharmacy Diversion Awareness Conference (PDAC)

	Individual pharmacies	**Chain pharmacy corporate offices**
Number of pharmacies that reported that they, or other representatives of their pharmacy or pharmacy chain, had not participated in a PDAC	122 of 162	9 of 32
Reason for not participating in a PDAC		
Not aware of the PDAC	93	3
A PDAC has not been offered in my state	5	2
Already participated in a PDAC prior to Jan. 1, 2012	0	0
A PDAC is scheduled in my state but has not yet taken place	1	0
A PDAC was held in my state but I was not able to attend	16	4
A PDAC was held in my state but I did not believe it would be helpful to me	3	0
Don't know	7	0
Other	4	1

Source: GAO surveys of DEA registrants. | GAO-15-471

Note: Between August 2014 and October 2014, we surveyed a generalizable random sample of DEA- registered individual pharmacies and we surveyed all of the corporate offices of the 38 chain pharmacies we identified using a DEA database. Registrants that reported that they had not participated in a PDAC could then provide responses for one or more reasons for not participating.

Table 17. Number of Registrants Reporting Perspectives on the Responsiveness of Drug Enforcement Administration (DEA) Headquarters and Field Office Staff

	Type of respondent	Not applicable – no inquiries	Very or moderately responsive	Slightly or not at all responsive	Don't know	Total responses
DEA headquarters staff	Distributors	49	48	8	2	**107**
	Individual pharmacies	10	26	5	3	**44**
	Chain pharmacy corporate offices	5	12	2	0	**19**
	Practitioners	7	7	3	3	**20**
DEA field office staff	Distributors	2	111	7	0	**120**
	Individual pharmacies	3	30	4	2	**39**
	Chain pharmacy corporate offices	2	22	3	0	**27**
	Practitioners	1	6	2	4	**13**

Source: GAO surveys of DEA registrants. | GAO-15-471

Notes: Between July 2014 and October 2014, we surveyed generalizable random samples of DEA- registered distributors, individual pharmacies, and practitioners, and we surveyed all of the corporate offices of the 38 chain pharmacies we identified using a DEA database. Registrants were asked a variation of a question specific to their registrant type about, in general, how responsive DEA headquarters and field office staff have been to registrants' inquiries about their roles and responsibilities.

Table 18. Number of Registrants Reporting Perspectives on the Courteousness and Respectfulness of Drug Enforcement Administration (DEA) Headquarters and Field Office Staff

	Type of respondent	Not applicable – no inquiries	Very or moderately courteous and respectful	Slightly or not at all courteous and respectful	Don't know	Total responses
DEA headquarters staff	Distributors	49	51	3	4	**107**
	Individual pharmacies	n/a	36	4	5	**45**
	Chain pharmacy corporate offices	n/a	15	2	1	**18**
	Practitioners	n/a	12	2	5	**19**
DEA field office staff	Distributors	0	114	6	1	**121**
	Individual pharmacies	n/a	34	4	1	**39**
	Chain pharmacy corporate offices	n/a	25	2	0	**27**
	Practitioners	n/a	6	2	4	**12**

Source: GAO surveys of DEA registrants. | GAO-15-471

Notes: Between July 2014 and October 2014, we surveyed generalizable random samples of DEA- registered distributors, individual pharmacies, and practitioners, and we surveyed all of the corporate offices of the 38 chain pharmacies we identified using a DEA database. Registrants were asked a variation of a question specific to their registrant type about how courteous and respectful DEA headquarters and field office staff have been towards them. An "n/a" indicates that the question or response was not offered to that registrant type.

Table 19. Number of Registrants Reporting Perspectives on the Discretion Shown by Drug Enforcement Administration (DEA) Headquarters and Field Office Staff in Handling Sensitive Information

	Type of respondent	**Not applicable – no sensitive information**	**Great or moderate discretion**	**Slight or no discretion**	**Don't know**	**Total responses**
DEA headquarters staff	Distributors	56	39	2	11	**108**
	Individual pharmacies	17	18	2	7	**44**
	Chain pharmacy corporate offices	3	10	1	5	**19**
	Practitioners	13	2	2	11	**28**
DEA field office staff	Distributors	10	97	3	10	**120**
	Individual pharmacies	10	24	2	3	**39**
	Chain pharmacy corporate offices	2	18	1	6	**27**
	Practitioners	5	3	1	4	13

Source: GAO surveys of DEA registrants. | GAO-15-471

Notes: Between July 2014 and October 2014, we surveyed generalizable random samples of DEA- registered distributors, individual pharmacies, and practitioners, and we surveyed all of the corporate offices of the 38 chain pharmacies we identified using a DEA database. Registrants were asked a variation of a question specific to their registrant type about, in general, how much discretion DEA headquarters and field office staff have shown in handling registrants' sensitive information.

Table 20. Number of Registrants Reporting Perspectives on the Helpfulness of Drug Enforcement Administration (DEA) Conferences, Initiatives, or Training

	Type of respondent	Very or moderately helpful	Slightly or not at all helpful	Don't know	Total responses
October 2013 Distributor Conference	Distributors	29	11	0	**40**
Distributor Initiative briefing	Distributors	15	3	0	**18**
Pharmacy Diversion Awareness Conferences (PDAC)	Individual pharmacies	24	3	0	**27**
	Chain pharmacy corporate offices	16	4	0	**20**
Other DEA conferences, initiatives, or training	Distributors	21	7	0	**28**
	Individual pharmacies	9	3	0	**12**
	Chain pharmacy corporate offices	9	1	0	**10**
	Practitioners	12	0	0	**12**

Source: GAO surveys of DEA registrants. | GAO-15-471

Notes: Between July 2014 and October 2014, we surveyed generalizable random samples of DEA- registered distributors, individual pharmacies, and practitioners, and we surveyed all of the corporate offices of the 38 chain pharmacies we identified using a DEA database. Registrants were asked a variation of a question specific to their registrant type about, in general, how helpful various DEA conferences, initiatives, or trainings have been in helping registrants understand their roles and responsibilities.

Table 21. Number of Registrants Reporting Perspectives on the Helpfulness of Various Drug Enforcement Administration (DEA) Guidance, Resources, and Tools

	Type of respondent	Very or moderately helpful	Slightly or not at all helpful	Don't know	Total responses
DEA's Know Your Customer guidance	Distributors	47	28	2	**77**
DEA's Pharmacist's Manual	Individual pharmacies	54	9	5	**68**
	Chain pharmacy corporate offices	20	2	0	**22**
DEA's Practitioner's Manual	Practitioners	30	3	2	**35**
DEA data or information on characteristics or trends in abuse and diversion	Distributors	56	22	0	**78**
	Individual pharmacies	43	11	3	**57**
	Chain pharmacy corporate offices	23	2	0	**25**
	Practitioners	32	14	3	49
Other DEA guidance, resources, or tools	Distributors	55	7	0	**62**
	Individual pharmacies	19	3	0	**22**
	Chain pharmacy corporate offices	14	1	0	**15**
	Practitioners	10	2	0	**12**

Source: GAO surveys of DEA registrants. | GAO-15-471

Notes: Between July 2014 and October 2014, we surveyed generalizable random samples of DEA- registered distributors, individual pharmacies, and practitioners, and we surveyed all of the corporate offices of the 38 chain pharmacies we identified using a DEA database. Registrants were asked a variation of a question specific to their registrant type about, in general, how helpful various DEA guidance, resources, and tools have been in helping registrants understand their roles and responsibilities.

Table 22. Chain Pharmacy Corporate Office Perspectives on Consistency of Responses among Drug Enforcement Administration (DEA) Field Offices

	Not applicable – no contact with staff in multiple DEA field offices	Very or moderately consistent	Slightly or not at all consistent	Don't know
Consistency of DEA field office responses	13	10	8	1

Source: GAO surveys of DEA registrants. | GAO-15-471

Note: Between August 2014 and October 2014, we surveyed all of the corporate offices of the 38 chain pharmacies we identified using a DEA database. Responses are from the 32 chain pharmacy corporate offices that responded to our survey. Chain pharmacy corporate offices were asked, "If you or other representatives of this pharmacy chain have been in contact with staff in multiple DEA field offices since Jan. 1, 2012, about your pharmacists' roles and responsibilities, in general, how consistent have their responses been?"

Table 23. Distributors' Perspectives on Changes to Business Practices and Influence of Drug Enforcement Administration (DEA) Enforcement Actions on Those Changes

	Has this facility made any of the following changes related to controlled substances since Jan. 1, 2012?			If yes: To what extent was this change influenced by DEA enforcement actions against registrants or as a result of the business climate those actions may have created?[a]		
	Yes	No	Don't know	Great or moderate extent	Slight or no extent	Don't know
Increased the number of questions we ask customers (e.g., pharmacies and practitioners) about their orders for controlled substances before filling the orders	66%(71)	33%	1%	42	27	1

	Has this facility made any of the following changes related to controlled substances since Jan. 1, 2012?			If yes: To what extent was this change influenced by DEA enforcement actions against registrants or as a result of the business climate those actions may have created?[a]		
	Yes	No	Don't know	Great or moderate extent	Slight or no extent	Don't know
Increased the number of times we delayed filling an order for controlled substances because the order appeared suspicious	48%(51)	49%	4%	37	14	0
Decided to place stricter thresholds on the quantity of controlled substances customers can order	57%(62)	40%	3%	52	10	0
Increased the number of times we denied orders for controlled substances because thresholds had been reached	43%(46)	50%	7%	34	11	0
Increased the number of times we dropped an existing customer because of suspicious orders	33%(36)	58%	9%	16	19	0
Increased the number of controlled substances that we have stopped disbursing because we learned they are frequently abused or diverted	20%(22)	72%	7%	12	10	0
Increased the security measures we take to prevent theft or diversion of controlled substances	54%(59)	44%	2%	39	20	0

Source: GAO surveys of DEA registrants. | GAO-15-471

Notes: Between August 2014 and October 2014, we surveyed a generalizable random sample of DEA-registered distributors. These percentage estimates of the entire population of distributor registrants are subject to margins of error of no more than ±10 percentage points. Percentages may not add to 100 percent because of rounding.

[a] The numbers of responses given to each of the seven extent questions represent only those responding "Yes" to the corresponding change question. Not all distributors responding "Yes" (number cited in parentheses) answered the corresponding extent question.

Table 24. Individual Pharmacies' Perspectives on Changes to Business Practices and Influence of Drug Enforcement Administration (DEA) Enforcement Actions on Those Changes

	Has this pharmacy made any of the following changes related to controlled substances since Jan. 1, 2012?			If yes: To what extent was this change influenced by DEA enforcement actions against registrants or as a result of the business climate those actions may have created?[a]		
	Yes	**No**	**Don't know**	**Great or moderate extent**	**Slight or no extent**	**Don't know**
Decreased the amount of controlled substances we order from our distributors	39% (63)	54%	7%	46	16	1
Increased the number of contacts we make to prescriber's offices to verify the legitimacy of prescriptions	71% (115)	23%	6%	85	28	1
Increase in the number of delays in filling prescriptions to check for legitimate medical need	58% (93)	34%	8%	63	28	0
Increase in the number of denials of prescription requests that couldn't be verified for legitimate medical needs	45% (72)	44%	11%	42	29	1

	Has this pharmacy made any of the following changes related to controlled substances since Jan. 1, 2012?			**If yes: To what extent was this change influenced by DEA enforcement actions against registrants or as a result of the business climate those actions may have created?[a]**		
	Yes	**No**	**Don't know**	**Great or moderate extent**	**Slight or no extent**	**Don't know**
Increased the number of questions we ask patients before filling questionable prescriptions to help ensure legitimate medical need	68% (110)	25%	7%	79	28	1
Decided to no longer dispense a specific controlled substance	24% (39)	69%	7%	25	13	1
Increased the number of checks we make with the state's Prescription Drug Monitoring Program prior to dispensing certain controlled substances to help ensure legitimate medical need	68% (109)	25%	8%	80	26	1

Source: GAO surveys of DEA registrants. | GAO-15-471

Notes: Between August 2014 and October 2014, we surveyed a generalizable random sample of DEA-registered individual pharmacies. These percentage estimates of the entire population of individual pharmacy registrants are subject to margins of error of no more than ±10 percentage points. Percentages may not add to 100 percent because of rounding.

[a] The numbers of responses given to each of the seven extent questions represent only those responding "Yes" to the corresponding change question. Not all Individual pharmacies responding "Yes" (number cited in parentheses) answered the corresponding extent question.

Table 25. Chain Pharmacy Corporate Offices' Perspectives on Changes to Business Practices and Influence of Drug Enforcement Administration (DEA) Enforcement Actions on Those Changes

	Has this pharmacy chain made any of the following changes related to controlled substances since Jan. 1, 2012?			If yes: To what extent was this change influenced by DEA enforcement actions against registrants or as a result of the business climate those actions may have created?[a]		
	Yes	**No**	**Don't know**	**Great or moderate extent**	**Slight or no extent**	**Don't know**
Decreased the amount of controlled substances we order from our distributors	71% (22)	16% (5)	13% (4)	17	5	0
Increased the number of contacts we make to prescriber's offices to verify the legitimacy of prescriptions	97% (31)	3% (1)	0	28	2	0
Increase in the number of delays in filling prescriptions to check for legitimate medical need	91% (29)	0	9% (3)	22	6	1
Increase in the number of denials of prescription requests that couldn't be verified for legitimate medical needs	84% (27)	6% (2)	9% (3)	19	8	0
Increased the number of questions we ask patients before filling questionable	97% (31)	0	3% (1)	26	3	1

	Has this pharmacy chain made any of the following changes related to controlled substances since Jan. 1, 2012?			If yes: To what extent was this change influenced by DEA enforcement actions against registrants or as a result of the business climate those actions may have created?[a]		
	Yes	**No**	**Don't know**	**Great or moderate extent**	**Slight or no extent**	**Don't know**
prescriptions to help ensure legitimate medical need						
Decided to no longer dispense a specific controlled substance	25% (8)	69% (22)	6% (2)	4	4	0
Increased the number of checks we make with the state's Prescription Drug Monitoring Program prior to dispensing certain controlled substances to help ensure legitimate medical need	87% (27)	3% (1)	10% (3)	19	6	1

Source: GAO surveys of DEA registrants. | GAO-15-471

Notes: Between August 2014 and October 2014, we surveyed all of the corporate offices of the 38 chain pharmacies we identified using a DEA database; responses are from the 32 chain pharmacy corporate offices that responded to our survey. We report both percentages and numbers (in parentheses) for the chain pharmacy corporate office responses because of the small population size. Percentages may not add to 100 percent because of rounding.

[a] The numbers of responses given to each of the seven extent questions represent only those responding "Yes" to the corresponding change question. Not all chain pharmacy corporate offices responding "Yes" (number cited in parentheses) answered the corresponding extent question.

Table 26. Practitioners' Perspectives on Changes to Business Practices and Influence of Drug Enforcement Administration (DEA) Enforcement Actions on Those Changes

	Have you made any of the following changes related to controlled substances since Jan. 1, 2012?			If yes: To what extent was this change influenced by DEA enforcement actions against registrants or as a result of the business climate those actions may have created?[a]		
	Yes	**No**	**Don't know**	**Great or moderate extent**	**Slight or no extent**	**Don't know**
Decreased the amount of controlled substances I prescribe, dispense, or administer	28%(49)	68%	5%	20	26	3
Increased the number of questions I ask patients before prescribing, dispensing, or administering certain controlled substances in order to help detect abuse or diversion	51%(90)	48%	1%	58	29	2
Decided to no longer prescribe, dispense, or administer a specific controlled substance	8%(14)	91%	1%	5	9	0
Decided to no longer provide addiction treatment services	3%(5)	17%	1%	2	3	0
Increased the number of checks I make with the state's Prescription Drug Monitoring Program prior to prescribing, dispensing, or administering certain controlled substances to help detect abuse or diversion	39%(67)	55%	7%	43	18	1

Source: GAO surveys of DEA registrants. | GAO-15-471

Notes: Between July 30, 2014 and October 14, 2014, we surveyed a generalizable random sample of DEA-registered practitioners. These percentage estimates of the entire population of practitioner registrants are subject to margins of error of no more than ±10 percentage points. Percentages may not add to 100 percent because of rounding.

[a] The numbers of responses given to each of the five extent questions represent only those responding "Yes" to the corresponding change question. Not all practitioners responding "Yes" (number cited in parentheses) answered the corresponding extent question.

Table 27. Percentage of Distributors That Were the Subject of Changes Made by Manufacturers, and the Extent to Which Those Changes Limited Access

	Have you experienced this?			If yes: To what extent has this limited your ability to meet your customers' needs?[a]		
	Yes	No	Don't know	Great or moderate extent	Slight or no extent	Don't know
Manufacturers have asked more questions regarding my orders	43% (34)	54%	4%	11	22	0
Manufacturers have put thresholds on the quantity of substances that I can order	38% (30)	54%	9%	10	18	0
Manufacturers have cancelled or suspended orders	15% (12)	80%	5%	4	7	0

Source: GAO surveys of Drug Enforcement Administration registrants. | GAO-15-471

Notes: Between August 2014 and October 2014, we surveyed a generalizable random sample of DEA-registered distributors. These percentage estimates of the entire population of distributor registrants are subject to margins of error of no more than ±10 percentage points. Percentages may not add to 100 percent because of rounding.

[a] The numbers of responses given to each of the three extent questions represent only those responding "Yes" to the corresponding change question. Not all distributors responding "Yes" (number cited in parentheses) answered the corresponding extent question.

Table 28. Percentage of Individual Pharmacies That Were the Subject of Changes Made by Distributors, and the Extent to Which Those Changes Limited Access

	Has your pharmacy experienced this?			If yes: To what extent has this limited your ability to dispense prescriptions for controlled substances?[a]		
	Yes	**No**	**Don't know**	**Great or moderate extent**	**Slight or no extent**	**Don't know**
Distributors have asked more questions regarding my orders	47%(66)	52%	1%	39	25	1
Distributors have put thresholds on the quantity of substances that my pharmacy can order	62%(87)	36%	3%	52	28	4
Distributors have cancelled or suspended orders from my pharmacy	25%(35)	75%	1%	20	14	1

Source: GAO surveys of Drug Enforcement Administration registrants. | GAO-15-471

Notes: Between August 2014 and October 2014, we surveyed a generalizable random sample of DEA-registered individual pharmacies. These percentage estimates of the entire population of individual pharmacy registrants are subject to margins of error of no more than ±10 percentage points. Percentages may not add to 100 percent because of rounding.

[a] The numbers of responses given to each of the three extent questions represent only those responding "Yes" to the corresponding change question. Not all Individual pharmacies responding "Yes" (number cited in parentheses) answered the corresponding extent question.

Table 29. Percentage of Chain Pharmacy Corporate Offices That Were the Subject of Changes Made by Distributors, and the Extent to Which Those Changes Limited Access

	Has your pharmacy chain experienced this?			If yes: To what extent has this limited your ability to dispense prescriptions for controlled substances?[a]		
	Yes	**No**	**Don't know**	**Great or moderate extent**	**Slight or no extent**	**Don't know**
Distributors have asked more questions regarding my pharmacy chain's orders	97% (31)	3% (1)	0	16	14	1
Distributors have put thresholds on the quantity of substances that my pharmacy chain can order	91% (29)	9% (3)	0	18	10	1
Distributors have cancelled or suspended orders from my pharmacy chain	81% (26)	19% (6)	0	6	19	1

Source: GAO surveys of Drug Enforcement Administration (DEA) registrants. | GAO-15-471

Notes: Between August 2014 and October 2014, we surveyed all of the corporate offices of the 38 chain pharmacies we identified using a DEA database; responses are from the 32 chain pharmacy corporate offices that responded to our survey. We report both percentages and numbers (in parentheses) for the chain pharmacy corporate office responses because of the small population size. Percentages may not add to 100 percent because of rounding.

[a] The numbers of responses given to each of the three extent questions represent only those responding "Yes" to the corresponding change question. Not all chain pharmacy corporate offices responding "Yes" (number cited in parentheses) answered the corresponding extent question.

Table 30. Percentage of Practitioners That Were the Subject of Changes Made by Pharmacies, and the Extent to Which Those Changes Limited Access

	Have you experienced this?			If yes: To what extent has this limited your patients' ability to obtain controlled substances for legitimate medical needs?[a]		
	Yes	**No**	**Don't know**	**Great or moderate extent**	**Slight or no extent**	**Don't know**
Pharmacies have asked increasing questions regarding my prescriptions for controlled substances	24% (41)	74%	2%	17	21	0
Pharmacies have delayed filling prescriptions I have written while they attempted to verify the legitimacy of the prescription	22% (38)	70%	8%	15	19	2
Pharmacies have denied filling certain prescriptions I have written for controlled substances	13% (22)	82%	5%	4	17	1

Source: GAO surveys of Drug Enforcement Administration registrants. | GAO-15-471

Notes: Between July 2014 and October 2014, we surveyed a generalizable random sample of DEA- registered practitioners. These percentage estimates of the entire population of practitioner registrants are subject to margins of error of no more than ±10 percentage points. Percentages may not add to 100 percent because of rounding.

[a] The numbers of responses given to each of the three extent questions represent only those responding "Yes" to the corresponding change question. Not all practitioners responding "Yes" (number cited in parentheses) answered the corresponding extent question.

APPENDIX III: DRUG ENFORCEMENT ADMINISTRATION (DEA) INVESTIGATIONS AND ENFORCEMENT ACTIONS DATA

Tables 31 through 38 show data on DEA investigations and enforcement actions from fiscal year 2009 through fiscal year 2013, focusing in particular on data related to DEA-registered distributors, pharmacies, and practitioners (including mid-level practitioners). As of September 2013, there were nearly 1.5 million registered distributors, pharmacies, and practitioners. DEA conducts investigations of its registrants as part of the registrant monitoring process and to ensure compliance with the Controlled Substances Act (CSA) and its implementing regulations. Following an investigation, DEA can initiate a variety of enforcement actions for violations of the CSA or its implementing regulations.

Table 31. Total Number of Drug Enforcement Administration (DEA) Scheduled Regulatory Investigations Initiated; Practitioners, Pharmacies, and Distributors, Fiscal Years 2009 – 2013

Registrant group	2009	2010	2011	2012	2013
All registrants and nonregistrants	1,212	3,863	4,691	4,893	6,171
Practitioners[a]	187	2,204	2,962	3,283	4,293
Pharmacies	15	11	18	28	97
Distributors[b]	168	275	263	256	302

Source: GAO analysis of DEA data. | GAO-15-471

Note: The reported number of scheduled regulatory investigations initiated does not include other regulatory activities such as pre-registration investigations, approvals of applications, withdrawals of applications, modifications of registration, and surrenders of registration.

[a] Practitioner totals include all categories of practitioners and mid-level practitioners for which DEA initiated a regulatory investigation.

[b] Chemical and reverse distributors were not included in these totals.

Table 32. Total Number of Drug Enforcement Administration (DEA) Complaint Investigations Initiated; Practitioners, Pharmacies, and Distributors, Fiscal Years 2009 – 2013

Registrant group	2009	2010	2011	2012	2013
All registrants and nonregistrants	907	869	1,222	1,414	1,428
Practitioners[a]	604	648	694	872	895
Pharmacies	99	113	250	360	383
Distributors[b]	10	16	22	21	29

Source: GAO analysis of DEA data. | GAO-15-471

[a] Practitioner totals include all categories of practitioners and mid-level practitioners for which DEA initiated a complaint investigation.

[b] Chemical and reverse distributors were not included in these totals.

Table 33. Total Number of Drug Enforcement Administration (DEA) Diversion- Related Criminal Investigations, Fiscal Years 2009 – 2013

	2009	2010	2011	2012	2013
Diversion-related criminal investigations	813	1,069	1,029	976	634

Source: GAO analysis of DEA data. | GAO-15-471

Note: The number of diversion-related criminal investigations only reflects those investigations linked to DEA's Defendant Statistical System arrest data.

Table 34. Total Number of Drug Enforcement Administration (DEA) Letters of Admonition; Practitioners, Pharmacies, and Distributors, Fiscal Years 2009 – 2013

Registrant group	2009	2010	2011	2012	2013
All registrants	394	694	1,052	1,231	1,296
Practitioners[a]	101	361	377	495	580
Pharmacies	114	48	268	364	338
Distributors[b]	30	31	50	49	64

Source: GAO analysis of DEA data. | GAO-15-471

[a] Practitioner totals include all categories of practitioners and mid-level practitioners for which DEA issued a Letter of Admonition, except for mid-level practitioner—animal shelter and military practitioners.

[b] Chemical and reverse distributors were not included in these totals.

Table 35. Total Number of Drug Enforcement Administration (DEA) Memoranda of Agreement; Practitioners, Pharmacies, and Distributors, Fiscal Years 2009 – 2013

Registrant group	2009	2010	2011	2012	2013
All registrants	135	141	212	286	340
Practitioners[a]	77	96	157	170	176
Pharmacies	34	14	30	99	131
Distributors[b]	5	4	1	3	7

Source: GAO analysis of DEA data. | GAO-15-471

[a] Practitioner totals include all categories of practitioners and mid-level practitioners for which DEA issued a Memoranda of Agreement, except for mid-level practitioner—animal shelter and military practitioners.

[b] Chemical and reverse distributors were not included in these totals.

Table 36. Total Number of Drug Enforcement Administration (DEA) Administrative Enforcement Hearings; Practitioners, Pharmacies, and Distributors, Fiscal Years 2009 – 2013

Registrant group	2009	2010	2011	2012	2013
All registrants	8	14	20	20	30
Practitioners[a]	5	7	8	11	9
Pharmacies	1	0	2	3	9
Distributors[b]	0	0	0	3	4

Source: GAO analysis of DEA data. | GAO-15-471

Notes: Administrative enforcement hearings, as reported here, reflect informal, administrative enforcement hearings conducted in the DEA field offices.

[a] Practitioner totals include all categories of practitioners and mid-level practitioners for which DEA held an administrative hearing.

[b] Reverse distributors were not included in these totals.

Table 37. Total Number of Drug Enforcement Administration (DEA) Orders to Show Cause and Immediate Suspension Orders, Fiscal Years 2009 – 2013

Type of administrative action	2009	2010	2011	2012	2013
Orders to show cause	74	67	66	50	45
Immediate suspension orders	28	40	65	41	16

Source: GAO analysis of DEA data. | GAO-15-471

Note: These data were not provided by registrant business code or subcode (e.g., practitioners, distributors).

Table 38. Number of Civil Fines and Total Fine Amounts for Violations of the Controlled Substances Act by Practitioners, Pharmacies, and Distributors, Fiscal Years 2009 – 2013

Practitioners[a]	**2009**	**2010**	**2011**	**2012**	**2013**
Total number of civil fines	35	27	42	39	38
Total amount	$1,229,295.00	$1,179,500.00	$1,288,800.00	$1,457,917.00	$1,404,934.00
Pharmacies	**2009**	**2010**	**2011**	**2012**	**2013**
Total number of civil fines	47	19	40	35	31
Total amount	$7,012,450.00	$2,160,736.00	$26,568,375.00	$56,504,041.00	$13,207,235.00
Distributors[b]	**2009**	**2010**	**2011**	**2012**	**2013**
Total number of civil fines	3	3	3	3	2
Total amount	$4,200,000.00	$73,496.00	$58,315,000.00	$ 493,276.00	$80,015,000.00

Source: GAO analysis of Drug Enforcement Administration data. | GAO-15-471

[a] Practitioner totals include all categories of practitioners and mid-level practitioners that paid a civil fine, except mid-level practitioner—animal shelter.

[b] Chemical and reverse distributors were not included in these totals.

End Notes

[1] Diversion can occur in a variety of ways, including as a result of illegal or improper prescribing, prescription forgery, pharmacy thefts, or "doctor shopping" where an individual—who may or may not have legitimate medical needs—goes to several doctors to obtain a prescription from each doctor. Diversion can also occur through illegal sales of prescription drugs, such as drugs sold by physicians, patients, or pharmacists, as well as individuals obtaining these substances without a valid prescription through Internet pharmacies or pain clinics.

[2] According to National Survey on Drug Use and Health data from 2012, about 20 percent of these people reported that they got the drug from one doctor and about 2 percent reported that they got the drug from more than one doctor. The other respondents reported getting the drug from sources such as the internet, a drug dealer, or by writing a fake prescription.

[3] Coalition Against Insurance Fraud, *Prescription for Peril: How Insurance Fraud Finances Theft and Abuse of Addictive Prescription Drugs* (Washington, D.C.: 2007), accessed March 18, 2015, http://www.insurancefraud.org/downloads/drugDiversion.pdf.

[4] Pub. L. No. 91-513, tit. II, 84 Stat. 1236, 1242-84 (codified as amended at 21 U.S.C. §§ 801-890, 901-971). According to the CSA, the term "controlled substance" means "a drug or other substance, or immediate precursor, included [in one of five classification schedules.]" A controlled substance is placed in a respective schedule based on whether it has a currently accepted medical use in treatment in the United States and its relative abuse potential and likelihood of causing dependence. The order of the schedules reflects substances that are progressively less dangerous and addictive. The term "controlled substance" as used in this report includes controlled prescription drugs such as opioid pain relievers. For simplicity, in this report, we use the term "prescription drugs" to refer to controlled prescription drugs.

[5] Practitioners, as used throughout this report, includes both those who DEA categorizes as practitioners for the purposes of registration, such as physicians, dentists, and podiatrists,

and those who DEA categorizes as mid-level practitioners for the purposes of registration, such as nurse practitioners, nurse anesthetists, and physician assistants.

[6] Department of Health and Human Services, Behavioral Health Coordinating Committee, Prescription Drug Abuse Subcommittee, *Addressing Prescription Drug Abuse in the United States: Current Activities and Future Opportunities* (Washington, D.C.: September 2013).

[7] Distributors purchase and store prescription drugs from manufacturers and sell them to customers such as pharmacies.

[8] The 26 national associations and other nonprofit organizations (referred to as national associations throughout this report) represent patients, practitioners, pharmacies and pharmacists, distributors, state regulatory authorities, state and local law enforcement, and drug manufacturers, among other relevant stakeholder types.

[9] Our results are generalizable to these populations of DEA registrants. Because we followed a probability procedure based on random selections, our samples are only three of a large number of samples that we might have drawn. As each sample could have provided different estimates, we express our confidence in the precision of our particular samples' results as 95 percent confidence intervals (e.g., from x to y percent). This is the interval that would contain the actual population value for 95 percent of the samples we could have drawn. As a result, we are 95 percent confident that each of the confidence intervals based on our survey includes the true values in the sample population.

[10] In our interviews with national pharmacy associations and in our survey pretests with selected chain pharmacies, we learned that the corporate offices of the larger chain pharmacies generally interact with federal agencies and other groups on issues related to prescription drug abuse and diversion as opposed to their individual pharmacy locations. Therefore, we sent a separate survey to the corporate offices for the chain pharmacies that we identified as having 50 or more registered stores so that the chain pharmacies could answer our survey on behalf of all of their stores.

[11] Estimates are subject to margins of error of no more than ±10 percentage points at the 95 percent confidence level, unless otherwise noted. American Association for Public Opinion Research response rate formula RR3 was used for practitioners, distributors, and individual pharmacies. RR1 was used for chain pharmacies. See American Association for Public Opinion Research, *Standard Definitions – Final Dispositions of Case Codes and Outcome Rates for Surveys*, accessed April 23, 2015, http://www.aapor.org/AAPORKentico/Communications/AAPOR-Journals/Standard- Definitions.aspx.

[12] Throughout this report, when referring to the registrants we surveyed, we regularly include chain pharmacy corporate offices, even though the chain pharmacy corporate office is not itself a DEA registrant. Instead, these offices represent 50 or more registered pharmacy locations. While they themselves are not a DEA registrant, they regularly interact with DEA on behalf of their registered pharmacy locations. Therefore, we refer to them in this context when discussing registrant perspectives.

[13] See GAO, *Standards for Internal Control in the Federal Government*, GAO/AIMD-00-21.3.1 (Washington, D.C.: Nov. 1999); and Drug Enforcement Administration, Office of Diversion Control, Customer Service Plan for Registrants, accessed February 18, 2015, http:// www.deadiversion.usdoj.gov/pubs/docs/cs_plan.htm.

[14] See GAO/AIMD-00-21.3.1.

[15] See 21 U.S.C. § 801, et seq.; see also 21 C.F.R. §§ 1300.01, et seq.

[16] Institute of Medicine of the National Academies, *Report Brief, Relieving Pain in America: A Blueprint for Transforming Prevention, Care, Education, and Research* (Washington, D.C.: National Academies Press, Revised 2012).

[17] For more information about the process through which DEA establishes controlled substances quotas, see GAO, *Drug Shortages: Better Management of the Quota Process for Controlled Substances Needed; Coordination between DEA and FDA Should Be Improved*, GAO-15-202 (Washington, D.C.: Feb. 2, 2015).

[18] 21 C.F.R. § 1301.74(b).

[19] 21 C.F.R. § 1306.04(a).

[20] 21 C.F.R. § 1306.04(a).

[21] According to DEA, the agency may also conduct general investigations of registrants, including pharmacies and physicians, such as pre-registration investigations to determine whether a pharmacy or physician is suitable to handle controlled substances and to obtain a DEA registration to do so, or modifications of registration. For example, for all new registration applications received from Florida pharmacies during the 2009 through 2013 time frame, DEA conducted a pre-registration general investigation.

[22] ARCOS is an automated reporting system used by DEA to monitor the flow of controlled substances from their point of manufacture to the point of sale or distribution at the dispensing/retail level such as hospitals, pharmacies, practitioners, and teaching institutions.

[23] The District of Columbia's prescription drug monitoring program is not yet operational. Missouri does not have a program.

[24] The types of practitioners who prescribe drugs vary among states. Physicians are the majority of covered practitioners, but in most states many nonphysicians also have prescribing authority, including physician assistants, dentists, optometrists, podiatrists, veterinarians, and certain types of nurses, such as nurse practitioners and advanced practice nurses.

[25] In our surveys, registrants were provided instructions specific to their registrant type asking them to provide information about their interactions with DEA since January 1, 2012, related to their roles and responsibilities for preventing prescription drug abuse and diversion under the CSA.

[26] Estimates cited throughout this report are subject to margins of error of no more than ±10 percentage points, unless otherwise noted.

[27] Information about upcoming conferences and meetings, as well as some past events, can be found on the DEA Office of Diversion Control website at http://www.deadiversion.usdoj.gov/mtgs/index.html, accessed March 12, 2015.

[28] According to DEA, the purpose of the 2013 Distributor Conference was to provide an overview of federal laws and regulations that affect pharmaceutical and chemical distributors, such as recordkeeping, ARCOS, and suspicious orders reporting. DEA noted that PDACs are designed to assist pharmacy personnel in identifying and preventing diversion activity. Each 1-day conference is open to pharmacy personnel (pharmacists, pharmacy technicians, or loss prevention personnel) who are employed by pharmacies or hospitals/clinics that are registered with DEA in the state in which the conference is being conducted. As of October 2014, when our surveys closed, DEA had held 44 PDACs in 21 states since 2011.

[29] According to DEA, every distributor was sent a notice of this conference by email, and for those emails that were rejected or returned, the agency attempted to contact the distributor via a different method.

[30] Since 2005, DEA has held Distributor Initiative briefings in order to educate and inform distributors and manufacturers of their due diligence responsibilities under the CSA. This is done by discussing a registrant's suspicious order monitoring system, reviewing their ARCOS data for sales and purchases of schedule II and III narcotics, and discussing national trends involving the abuse of controlled substances. DEA reported that as of January 2014 the agency had met with 82 corporations representing 276 individual registrants.

[31] See GAO/AIMD-00-21.3.1.

[32] This estimate for individual pharmacies has a margin of error of ±14 percentage points.

[33] See GAO/AIMD-00-21.3.1.

[34] Distributors were asked the question, "Based on your use of DEA's Know Your Customer guidance, how helpful is it for understanding your roles and responsibilities?"

[35] See GAO/AIMD-00-21.3.1.

[36] Schedules of Controlled Substances: Rescheduling of Hydrocodone Combination Products from Schedule III to Schedule II, 79 Fed. Reg. 49661 (2014). The CSA places each controlled substance in one of five schedules based on whether the substance has a currently accepted medical use in treatment in the United States, its relative potential for abuse, and the degree

of dependence the drug or other substance may cause. For example, schedule I controlled substances, such as heroin and LSD, have a high potential for abuse and no currently accepted medical use in treatment in the United States, while schedule II controlled substances such as oxycodone have a high potential for abuse that may lead to severe psychological or physical dependence, but also have a currently accepted medical use. Schedule III substances have currently accepted medical uses and a potential for abuse that may lead to moderate or low physical dependence or high psychological dependence.

[37] DEA Tactical Diversion Squads are teams of DEA diversion personnel, as well as other federal, state, and local law enforcement personnel, whose mission is to detect, investigate, disrupt, and refer for prosecution violators of federal and state controlled substance statutes pertaining to drug diversion.

[38] DEA began hosting National Prescription Drug Take-Back events in 2010.

[39] Meetings include conferences, forums, and summits related to prescription drug abuse and diversion.

[40] Disposal of Controlled Substances, 77 Fed. Reg. 75784-01 (2012). DEA's rulemaking was to implement the Secure and Responsible Drug Disposal Act of 2010, which amended the CSA to expand the options available to patients to dispose of unneeded prescription drugs beyond destroying them or giving them to law enforcement. Among other things, DEA's final rule, which took effect October 9, 2014, allows manufacturers, distributors, and retail pharmacies to become authorized collectors of unused or unwanted controlled substances for disposal purposes.79 Fed. Reg. 53520-01 (2014).

[41] While investigations are not themselves enforcement actions, they may lead to enforcement actions; for example, if noncompliance issues are found during an investigation DEA may issue a letter of admonition. Further, our survey results suggest that registrants may change certain business practices as a result of an investigation, or fear of becoming the target of an investigation. Therefore, we included data on DEA investigations in our analyses.

[42] See GAO, *Prescription Drug Control: DEA Has Enhanced Efforts to Combat Diversion, but Could Better Assess and Report Program Results*, GAO-11-744 (Washington D.C.: Aug. 26, 2011).

[43] In the survey questions we asked registrants to consider how, if at all, DEA enforcement actions, or the possibility of actions, against DEA registrants has affected them and the business climate in which they and others in the prescription drug supply chain operate.

[44]See GAO/AIMD-00-21.3.1.

[45] For the purposes of this report, the stakeholders whose perspectives we obtained include DEA registrants (distributors, pharmacies, and practitioners), state government officials in four states, and officials from 26 national associations and nonprofits representing various interests.

[46] Federal government registrants were excluded from our survey target populations as our review was focused only on nonfederal stakeholders' interactions with DEA.

[47] In our interviews with national pharmacy associations and in our survey pretests with selected chain pharmacies, we learned that the corporate offices of the larger chain pharmacies generally interact with federal agencies and other groups on issues related to prescription drug abuse and diversion as opposed to their individual pharmacy locations. Therefore, we sent a separate survey to the corporate offices for the chain pharmacies that we identified as having 50 or more registered stores so that the chain pharmacies could answer our survey on behalf of all of their stores.

[48] While we originally identified a population of more than 50 chain pharmacies that had 50 or more registered pharmacy locations, we arrived at the smaller number of 38 through a manual process that involved determining corporate family membership and combining subsidiary pharmacy chains with their parent corporations.

[49] See GAO, *Standards for Internal Control in the Federal Government*, GAO/AIMD-00-21.3.1 (Washington, D.C.: Nov. 1999); and Drug Enforcement Administration, Office of Diversion

Control, Customer Service Plan for Registrants, accessed February 18, 2015, http://www.deadiversion.usdoj.gov/pubs/docs/cs_plan.htm.

[50] Some of the state agencies had overlapping responsibilities; for example, a state regulatory board may also be the state's Controlled Substances Authority. In addition, state officials with New York's pharmacy board and office that investigates complaints about practitioners declined to be interviewed for our study.

[51] We interviewed officials from the following 26 national associations: the National Association of State Alcohol and Drug Directors, the Healthcare Distribution Management Association, the National Association of Chain Drug Stores, the Federation of State Medical Boards, the National Alliance of State Pharmacy Associations, the National Community Pharmacists Association, the International Association of Chiefs of Police, the American Academy of Pain Management, the National Sheriffs' Association, the Major Cities Chiefs Association, the National Association of Boards of Pharmacy, the Center for Lawful Access and Abuse Deterrence, the National Association of Attorneys General, the National Association of State Controlled Substances Authorities, the National Governor's Association, the American Cancer Society's Cancer Action Network, the American Medical Association, the Alliance of States with Prescription Monitoring Programs, the Pharmaceutical Research and Manufacturers of America, the Generic Pharmaceutical Association, the National Association of Drug Diversion Investigators, The Partnership at Drugfree.org, the Association of State and Territorial Health Officials, the National Hospice and Palliative Care Organization, the Center for Safe Internet Pharmacies, and the Express Delivery and Logistics Association.

[52] See GAO/AIMD-00-21.3.1.

In: Prescription Drugs and the DEA
Editor: Kara Morris
ISBN: 978-1-63484-606-6

Chapter 2

THE CONTROLLED SUBSTANCES ACT: REGULATORY REQUIREMENTS*

Brian T. Yeh

SUMMARY

This report highlights certain non-criminal regulatory requirements of the Controlled Substances Act (CSA). The CSA and its implementing regulations establish a framework through which the federal government regulates the use of controlled substances for legitimate medical, scientific, research, and industrial purposes, and prevents these substances from being diverted for illegal purposes. The CSA assigns various plants, drugs, and chemicals (such as narcotics, stimulants, depressants, hallucinogens, and anabolic steroids) to one of five schedules based on the substance's medical use, potential for abuse, and safety or dependence liability. Schedule I contains substances that have no currently accepted medical use and cannot safely be made available to the public under a prescription, while Schedules II, III, IV, and V include substances that have recognized medical uses and may be manufactured, distributed, and used in accordance with the CSA. The order of the schedules reflects substances that are progressively less dangerous and addictive. To

* This is an edited, reformatted and augmented version of the Congressional Research Service Publication, CRS Report for Congress RL34635, dated December 13, 2012.

restrict access to chemicals used in the illicit manufacture of certain controlled substances, the CSA also regulates 40 "listed chemicals." Furthermore, the CSA regulates controlled substance "analogues," which are substances that are not controlled but are structurally or pharmacologically similar to substances found in Schedule I or II and have no accepted medical use.

Unless specifically exempted by the CSA, any person who handles controlled substances or listed chemicals (such as drug manufacturers, wholesale distributors, doctors, hospitals, pharmacies, and scientific researchers) must register with the Drug Enforcement Administration (DEA) in the U.S. Department of Justice, which administers and enforces the CSA. Registrants must keep accurate and complete records of all transactions involving controlled substances, maintain detailed inventories of the substances in their possession, and periodically file reports with the DEA, as well as ensure that controlled substances are securely stored and safeguarded in accordance with DEA regulations.

Between 10%-11% of all drug prescriptions written in the United States are for pharmaceutical controlled substances. Only licensed medical practitioners (who are registered with the DEA) are authorized to prescribe controlled substances listed in Schedules II-V to patients; such prescriptions may only be issued by a practitioner who is "acting in the usual course of his professional practice," and for a "legitimate medical purpose." The CSA authorizes the DEA Administrator to suspend or revoke a physician's prescription privileges upon a finding that he has "committed such acts as would render his registration ... inconsistent with the public interest."

While the CSA provides criminal sanctions for *illicit* possession, manufacture, or distribution of controlled substances, the statute also contains a few noteworthy penalty provisions that are specifically applicable to persons who are authorized by the DEA to handle controlled substances lawfully. The CSA sets forth certain offenses involving listed chemicals and DEA registration and other prohibited acts relating to registrants who manufacture, distribute, and dispense controlled substances.

The Controlled Substances Act (CSA or the act)[1] is the statutory framework through which the federal government regulates the lawful production, possession, and distribution of controlled substances. The CSA places various plants, drugs, and chemicals (such as narcotics, stimulants, depressants, hallucinogens, and anabolic steroids) into one of five schedules based on the substance's medical use, potential for abuse, and safety or dependence liability. Further, the act requires persons who handle controlled substances or listed chemicals (such as drug manufacturers, wholesale distributors, doctors, hospitals, pharmacies, and scientific researchers) to register with the Drug Enforcement Administration (DEA) in the U.S. Department of Justice, which administers and enforces the CSA. Registrants must maintain detailed records of their respective controlled substance inventories as well as establish adequate security controls to minimize theft and diversion.[2] Although the CSA sets forth criminal provisions[3] for the unlawful manufacture, possession, and distribution of controlled substances, this report will instead focus on the act's non-criminal regulatory requirements[4] for those who legitimately produce, distribute, and dispense controlled substances.

FORMAL SCHEDULING

The placement of drugs or other substances into schedules under the CSA is based upon the substance's medical use, potential for abuse, and safety or dependence liability.[5] The act further provides a mechanism for substances to be controlled,[6] or added to a schedule; decontrolled, or removed from the scheduling framework altogether; and rescheduled or transferred from one schedule to another.[7]

The proceedings to add, delete, or change the schedule of a drug or substance may be initiated by the DEA, the U.S. Department of Health and Human Services (HHS), or by petition by any interested person.[8] When a petition is received by the DEA, the agency initiates its own investigation of the drug or substance. The DEA may also initiate an investigation at any time in response to information received from law enforcement laboratories, state and local law enforcement and regulatory agencies, or other sources of information.

After the DEA's initial investigation, the DEA Administrator (Administrator)[9] requests from the Assistant Secretary of Health of HHS (Assistant Secretary of Health) a scientific and medical evaluation and recommendation as to whether the drug or substance should be controlled or removed from control.[10] The Assistant Secretary of Health in turn solicits information from the Commissioner of the Food and Drug Administration, and obtains evaluations and recommendations from the National Institute on Drug Abuse. The Assistant Secretary of Health then consolidates the requested information and transmits back to the DEA a medical and scientific evaluation regarding the drug or substance, along with a recommendation as to whether the drug or substance should be controlled and into which schedule it should be placed.[11]

The Administrator then evaluates all of the relevant data and makes a final determination as to whether the drug or substance should be controlled or removed entirely from control.[12] In making a determination regarding the control of a drug or substance, the Administrator must consider factors such as the drug's actual or relative potential for abuse; scientific evidence of its pharmacological effect; the current state of scientific knowledge regarding the drug or substance; the risk to the public health; and whether the substance is an immediate precursor of a substance already controlled under the act.[13] After the Administrator makes such a determination, he must make specific findings concerning the drug or substance that dictate the schedule in which the drug or substance will be placed.[14]

Congress may also add a substance to a schedule through legislation.

Emergency or Temporary Scheduling

The CSA was amended by the Comprehensive Crime Control Act of 1984[15] to include a provision allowing the Administrator to place a drug or substance, on a temporary basis, into Schedule I when necessary to avoid an "imminent hazard to public safety."[16] The Administrator, however, may not issue a temporary scheduling order until thirty days after he notifies both the public and the HHS Secretary of his intent to issue the temporary scheduling order and of his justification for issuing the order.[17] Further, the Administrator must consider any of the HHS Secretary's comments regarding the temporary order.[18]

When issuing a temporary scheduling order, the Administrator must consider, with respect to the finding of an imminent hazard to public safety (i) the history of the drug or substance and its current pattern of abuse; (ii) the scope, duration, and significance of the drug or substance's abuse; (iii) the risk to public health; (iv) diversion of the drug or substance from legitimate channels; and (v) the drug or substance's "clandestine importation, manufacture, or distribution."[19] A drug or substance may be temporarily scheduled for two years and possibly longer—up to an additional year—if formal scheduling procedures have been initiated.[20] This emergency scheduling applies only to substances with no accepted medical use in the United States.

Listed Chemicals

In an effort to restrict access to chemicals used in the illicit manufacture of certain controlled substances in violation of the CSA, Congress passed the Chemical Diversion and Trafficking Act (CDTA) in 1988.[21] The CDTA and its subsequent amendments[22] allow the DEA to control 40 chemicals[23] and restrict their diversion. These 40 chemicals are referred to by the CSA as "listed chemicals."[24] Listed chemicals are divided into two categories: List I[25] and List II.[26] While both categories of chemicals can be used to illicitly manufacture controlled substances, List I chemicals are more strenuously regulated than List II chemicals because List I chemicals are "important to the manufacture of a controlled substance."[27]

Controlled Substances Analogues

Controlled substance analogues are substances that are not controlled but are structurally or pharmacologically similar to substances found in Schedule I or II and have no accepted medical use.[28] A substance that meets the definition of the term "controlled substance analogue" and is intended for human consumption is treated as if it were a controlled substance in Schedule I.[29] Controlled substance analogues are different from listed chemicals because such analogues are typically intended for human consumption as a substitute for a controlled substance, whereas listed chemicals are not intended for human consumption but are instead used as "ingredients" in the manufacture of certain controlled substances.

Synthetic Drugs

Synthetic drugs are chemically produced in a laboratory; their chemical structure can be either identical to or different from naturally occurring drugs, and their effects are designed to mimic or even enhance those of natural drugs.[30] Many synthetic cathinones (central nervous system stimulants) are marketed under household names such as "bath salts" or "plant food" and are stamped with the warning "not intended for human consumption." This action is intended to circumvent the CSA's statutory definition of a controlled substance analogue. In October 2011, the DEA used its temporary scheduling authority to place three synthetic cathinones on Schedule I of the CSA.[31] In June 2012, Congress passed the Synthetic Drug Abuse Prevention Act of 2012—Subtitle D of Title XI of the Food and Drug Administration Safety and Innovation Act (P.L. 112-144)—which permanently added two of these synthetic cathinones to Schedule I of the CSA, along with cannabimimetic substances (commonly referred to as synthetic marijuana).[32]

International Treaty Obligations

The United States is a party to the Single Convention on Narcotic Drugs of 1961, which was designed to establish effective control over international and domestic traffic in narcotics, coca leaf, cocaine, and marijuana. The United States is also party to the Convention on Psychotropic Substances of 1971, which was designed to establish similar control over stimulants, depressants, and hallucinogens. Treaty obligations may require the Attorney General to control or reschedule a substance if existing controls are less stringent than those required by a treaty.[33]

REGULATION

The CSA creates a "closed system" of distribution[34] in which distribution may lawfully occur among registered handlers of controlled substances, referred to as "registrants."[35] Central to this closed system of distribution is the registration of all persons or entities authorized by the DEA to handle controlled substances. The DEA has described the movement of a controlled substance from manufacture to the patient as follows:

> [A] controlled substance, after being manufactured by a DEA-registered manufacturer, may be transferred to a DEA-registered distributor for subsequent distribution to a DEA- registered retail pharmacy. After a DEA-registered practitioner, such as a physician or a dentist, issues a prescription for a controlled substance to a patient (i.e., the ultimate user), that patient can fill that prescription at a retail pharmacy to obtain that controlled substance. In this system, the manufacturer, the distributor, the practitioner, and the retail pharmacy are all required to be DEA registrants, or to be exempted from the requirement of registration, to participate in the process.[36]

All registrants are required by the CSA to maintain complete and accurate inventories and records of all regulated transactions involving controlled substances and listed chemicals, as well as provide adequate security controls to prevent their diversion. Therefore, a particular controlled substance is always under the control of a DEA-registered person until it reaches the patient or is destroyed, and the CSA's regulatory requirements "ensure that all controlled substances are accounted for from their creation until their dispensing or destruction."[37]

Registration

The CSA defines who must register with the DEA in order to handle controlled substances.[38] Every person who manufactures, distributes, dispenses, imports, or exports any controlled substance, or who proposes to engage in the manufacture, distribution, dispensing, importation, or exportation of any controlled substance, must register with the DEA, unless they are exempt.[39] Generally, all manufacturers, distributors, and practitioners who deal with controlled substances must register. The CSA refers to an individual patient as an "ultimate user," which it defines as "a person who has lawfully obtained, and who possesses, a controlled substance for his own use or for the use of a member of his household or for an animal owned by him or by a member of his household."[40] Ultimate users are not required to register with the DEA[41] because the controlled substances in their possession "are no longer part of the closed system of distribution and are no longer subject to DEA's system of corresponding accountability."[42]

Manufacturers and distributors of controlled substances must register with the DEA annually, and those who dispense controlled substances must obtain registrations that may not be issued for less than one year or more than three years.[43] Any person who is required to register in order to manufacture, distribute, or dispense controlled substances, but has not yet registered, may apply for registration at any time.[44] Those who already are registered can apply for re-registration not more than 60 days before the expiration date of their current registration.[45] Registrations specify the extent to which registrants are authorized to manufacture, possess, distribute, or dispense controlled substances. The Administrator is authorized to charge reasonable fees relating to the registration and control of the manufacturing, distribution, and dispensing of controlled substances under the act.[46] In addition, the

Administrator can inspect the establishments of registrants or applicants for registration.[47]

Registration is granted to applicants only if it would be consistent with the "public interest" to do so.[48] The Administrator uses several criteria to assess whether registering an applicant is consistent with the "public interest." The criteria differ depending on the substance involved and whether the applicant is a manufacturer, distributor, or practitioner, but generally include factors such as those relating to public health and safety and compliance with state and local laws.[49]

The Administrator also has the authority to deny, revoke, or suspend registrations under certain circumstances but must provide adequate grounds for doing so.[50] Before the DEA can deny an application, the agency must provide the applicant with an opportunity to demonstrate why the registration should not be denied.[51] However, the Administrator can suspend without notice any registration in order to avoid imminent danger to public health and safety.[52] A revocation or suspension of a registration may be applicable to a particular controlled substance or class of controlled substances. For example, a manufacturer who has been found to have violated the registration provisions regarding a Schedule II substance will still be able to manufacture controlled substances in Schedules III-V because the revocation or suspension relates only to one class of controlled substances.[53]

The registration of an individual terminates when the person dies, ceases legal existence, or discontinues business or professional practice.[54] A registrant who ceases legal existence or discontinues business or professional practice must notify the DEA promptly of this occurrence. A registration cannot be transferred to someone else unless the Administrator provides his express, written consent for such a transfer to occur.[55]

In some instances, applicants must apply for several separate registrations in order to comply with the CSA. Separate registrations are required for each principal place of business or professional practice where controlled substances are manufactured, distributed, imported, exported, or dispensed.[56] For example, a physician who is regularly engaged in dispensing controlled substances at one location must register to dispense controlled substances at other locations if he chooses to dispense controlled substances at these other locations.[57] However, with the enactment of the Ryan Haight Online Pharmacy Consumer Protection Act of 2008, the DEA Administrator must modify existing registrations of pharmacies to authorize them to dispense controlled substances by means of the Internet, unless the Administrator determines that such modification would be inconsistent with the public interest.[58]

Recordkeeping Requirements

In addition to registration requirements, the CSA contains several recordkeeping provisions.[59] A registrant authorized to handle controlled substances must keep accurate records and maintain detailed inventories in compliance with applicable federal and state law. For example, a registrant must maintain a complete and accurate record of each substance manufactured, received, sold, delivered, or otherwise disposed of by the registrant.[60] Furthermore, inventories must be available for inspection for at least two years.[61] These records are generally open for inspection by federal authorities and state officers tasked with enforcing state narcotics laws.[62] The CSA declares that is unlawful for any person to "refuse or negligently fail to make, keep, or furnish any record, report, notification, declaration, order or order form, statement, invoice, or information required" by the CSA;[63] it is also unlawful for any person knowingly or intentionally "to furnish false or fraudulent material information in, or omit any material information from, any application, report, record, or other document required to be made, kept, or filed" under the CSA.[64]

Certain DEA regulations implementing the CSA also apply to listed chemicals.[65] For example, all registrants authorized to handle listed chemicals (List I and List II) must maintain records of regulated transactions and submit various reports to the DEA.[66] However, the Administrator has the authority to exempt specified concentrations of listed chemical mixtures from the recordkeeping requirements set forth in section 830 of the act that require registrants to maintain detailed records of every regulated transaction.[67]

Distribution

As a means to ensure that only authorized registrants obtain Schedule I and II drugs from manufacturers and distributors, the CSA requires registrants who legitimately distribute[68] controlled substances or listed chemicals to keep records of shipments to purchasers.[69] Manufacturers and distributors must receive a special order form from a purchaser prior to shipping Schedule I and II drugs.[70] The form is preprinted by the DEA with the name and address of the purchaser and the drugs must be shipped by the supplier filling the order to the purchaser's registered location.[71] All manufacturers must forward copies of completed order forms to the DEA by the close of the month in which the shipment is made.[72] The CSA also provides for electronic orders of Schedule I and II drugs.[73] Manufacturers must also forward copies of filled electronic orders to the DEA within 2 business days.[74]

The DEA further monitors the distribution of controlled substances by requiring manufacturers and distributors of Schedule I and II drugs to file reports[75] through the Automated Reports and Consolidated Orders System (ARCOS).[76] Certain narcotics listed in Schedules III and IV are also covered by the ARCOS reporting requirements.[77]

Registered pharmacies that are authorized to dispense controlled substances by means of the Internet must report to the DEA Administrator the total quantity of each controlled substance that the pharmacy has dispensed each month.[78] In addition, online pharmacies[79] must clearly display on their website homepage a statement that they comply with federal and state law concerning the delivery or sale of controlled substances, as well as post certain disclosure information such as

- the name and address of the pharmacy as it appears on the pharmacy's DEA registration certificate,
- the pharmacy's telephone number and email address,
- a list of states in which the pharmacy is licensed to dispense controlled substance,
- the identification and contact information of the pharmacist-in-charge, and
- the following statement: "This online pharmacy will only dispense a controlled substance to a person who has a valid prescription issued for a legitimate medical purpose based upon a medical relationship with a prescribing practitioner. This includes at least one prior in-person medical evaluation or medical evaluation via telemedicine in accordance with applicable requirements of section 309."[80]

An online pharmacy must notify the DEA Administrator, and the state boards of pharmacy in any states in which the online pharmacies operate, thirty days before offering a controlled substance for sale, delivery, distribution, or dispensing; such notification must include pharmacy's Internet site address, the information that is required to be posted on the pharmacy's website, and the DEA registration numbers of the pharmacy and practitioners who work for it.[81] Online pharmacies that were already operational as of April 13, 2009, had to submit this notification to the DEA Administrator and any applicable state boards of pharmacy no later than May 12, 2009.

Dispensing to Patients

The CSA further provides special control mechanisms for licensed practitioners and pharmacists who dispense[82] controlled substances in Schedules II-V to patients for legitimate medical purposes. Because controlled substances classified as Schedule I drugs are deemed to have no accepted medical purpose in the United States, they may only be used for research, and practitioners may not prescribe them to patients. Under the CSA, only licensed medical practitioners[83] are authorized to prescribe controlled substances listed in Schedules II-V to patients.[84] A prescription for a controlled substance must be "issued for a legitimate medical purpose by an individual practitioner acting in the usual course of his professional practice."[85] Accordingly, practitioners have a responsibility to ensure that the controlled substance is properly prescribed and dispensed.[86]

No controlled substance in Schedules II may be dispensed to a patient by a pharmacist without a written prescription[87] from a practitioner, except in certain cases where the practitioner administers the controlled substance directly to the patient.[88] However, in the case of an emergency situation, a practitioner may orally authorize a pharmacist to fill a prescription for a Schedule II controlled substance. DEA regulations define "emergency situation" as those in which the prescribing practitioner determines:[89]

1. that immediate administration of the controlled substance is necessary, for proper treatment of the intended ultimate user; and
2. that no appropriate alternative treatment is available, including administration of a drug which is not a controlled substance under schedule II of the act; and
3. that it is not reasonably possible for the prescribing practitioner to provide a written prescription to be presented to the person dispensing the substance, prior to the dispensing.

Such an emergency oral authorization for a Schedule II substance may be filled by a pharmacist if the following conditions are met:[90]

1. the quantity of the drug prescribed and dispensed is limited to an amount adequate to treat the patient during the emergency period;
2. the prescription is immediately reduced to writing by the pharmacist and contains all the information that federal regulations require of

prescriptions,[91] except for the signature of the prescribing individual practitioner;

3. if the prescribing individual practitioner is not known to the pharmacist, he must make a reasonable effort to determine that the oral authorization came from a registered individual practitioner, which may include a callback to the prescribing individual practitioner using his phone number as listed in the telephone directory and/or other good faith efforts to insure his identity; and
4. within seven days after authorizing an emergency oral prescription, the prescribing individual practitioner must deliver a written prescription to the dispensing pharmacist. The practitioner must write on the face of the prescription "Authorization for Emergency Dispensing" and also write the date of the oral order. Upon receipt, the dispensing pharmacist must attach this paper prescription to the oral emergency prescription that had earlier been reduced to writing. The pharmacist must notify the nearest DEA office if the prescribing individual practitioner fails to deliver a written prescription to him; failure of the pharmacist to do so shall void the authority to dispense without a written prescription of a prescribing individual practitioner.

Controlled substances in Schedules III-V may be dispensed by a pharmacy pursuant to either a written or oral prescription, including a facsimile of a written prescription;[92] these substances may also be administered or dispensed directly by the practitioner in the course of his professional practice without a prescription.[93]

Practitioners are permitted to sign and transmit electronic prescriptions for controlled substances, assuming that the electronic prescription complies with detailed requirements set forth in the applicable federal regulations.[94]

Pharmacists may partially fill a prescription for Schedule II substances under certain circumstances.[95] Pharmacists are prohibited from refilling prescriptions for Schedule II substances.[96] Prescriptions for controlled substances in Schedules III and IV, however, may be filled or refilled by pharmacists up to five times within six months after the date on which the prescription was issued, unless the prescribing practitioner authorizes a renewal of the prescription.[97] A pharmacy may process electronic prescriptions for controlled substances if it has satisfied several conditions described in the applicable federal regulations.[98]

A controlled substance that is a prescription drug may not be delivered, distributed, or dispensed by means of the Internet without a "valid prescription."[99] Only with respect to this provision of the Controlled Substances Act, a "valid prescription" means a prescription that is issued for a legitimate medical purpose in the usual course of professional practice by a practitioner who has conducted at least one medical evaluation of the patient in the physical presence of the practitioner.[100]

Quotas

The DEA limits the quantity of Schedule I and II controlled substances which may be produced in a given calendar year. The CSA authorizes the Administrator to

- establish aggregate production quotas for all manufacturers;
- establish individual production quotas for specific registered manufactures;
- establish individual production quotas for registrants who have not manufactured controlled substances during one or more proceeding years; and
- implement quota increases for individual manufacturers where necessary.[101]

By regulation, the Administrator must consider the following factors in making his quota determinations: (i) the total disposal of the controlled substance during the current and two preceding years; (ii) trends in the national rate of new disposal of the controlled substance; (iii) total inventories (actual or estimated) of "the class and all substances manufactured from the class [of controlled substances listed in Schedule I or II];" (iv) projected demand for a particular controlled substance; and (v) other relevant factors affecting the use of controlled substances including, changes in the currently accepted medical use of a controlled substance, the economic and physical availability of the raw materials necessary to produce a controlled substance, and recent unforeseen emergencies (i.e., natural disasters).[102]

Security

For the purposes of ensuring the secure storage and distribution of controlled substances and listed chemicals, all applicants and registrants must generally "provide effective controls and procedures to guard against theft and diversion of controlled substances."[103] DEA regulations further require all applicants and registrants to substantially comply with specific security standards for storage of controlled substances and List I chemicals.[104] Applicants and registrants must also be prepared to make adjustments to their security systems in the event that a controlled substance is transferred to another schedule or removed from control under the CSA.[105]

DEA regulations also detail specific security requirements for the different types of applicants and registrants. For example, non-practitioners (i.e., manufacturers, distributors, and narcotic treatment programs) are required to store Schedule I and II substances in electronically monitored safes, steel cabinets or vaults that meet or exceed certain specifications.[106] Licensed practitioners must store controlled substances in a "securely locked, substantially constructed cabinet"[107] and must notify the DEA of the theft or significant loss of any controlled substances within one business day of discovering such loss or theft.[108] Furthermore, all practitioners are prohibited from hiring employees who have been convicted of a drug-related felony or who have had a DEA registration denied or revoked.[109] DEA regulations recommend that non-practitioners carefully screen individuals before hiring them as employees, to ensure that job applicants do not have convictions for crimes or have engaged in unauthorized use of controlled substances.[110]

Disposal of Controlled Substances[111]

DEA registrants may need to dispose of controlled substances in their possession when they are expired, damaged, contaminated, or otherwise unwanted. Under the CSA and DEA regulations, there are three different options for registrants to dispose of controlled substances:[112]

1. The distributor or dispenser may return the controlled substance to the pharmaceutical manufacturer who accepts returns of outdated or damaged controlled substances.
2. The distributor, dispenser, or manufacturer may itself dispose of the controlled substances under procedures specified by federal regulation.[113]
3. The distributor, dispenser, or manufacturer may transfer the controlled substances to a "reverse distributor" to take custody of the controlled

substances for the purpose of returning them to the manufacturer or arranging for their disposal.[114]

Penalties

While the criminal provisions of the CSA focus mainly on the *illicit* possession, manufacture, and distribution of controlled substances,[115] there are a few noteworthy penalty provisions applicable to persons registered with the DEA. The CSA sets forth certain offenses involving listed chemicals,[116] DEA registration,[117] and other prohibited acts related to registrants who manufacture, distribute and dispense controlled substances.[118]

With respect to DEA registration generally, registrants authorized to distribute or dispense any controlled substance are prohibited from distributing, dispensing, or manufacturing controlled substances that are not authorized by a registrant's registration.[119] Registrants must maintain accurate records and furnish them when required to do so by law enforcement officials.[120] Registrants must also maintain a degree of transparency by allowing law enforcement officials access to their premises for inspections authorized by the CSA.[121] Failure to adhere to the registration requirements of the CSA may subject a registrant to civil fines, imprisonment, or both.[122]

The CSA also proscribes certain acts related to the manufacture and distribution of controlled substances and listed chemicals. Registrants who knowingly or intentionally (i) distribute Schedule I and II substances without a valid order form;[123] (ii) use an invalid registration number during the course of handling or acquiring controlled substances;[124] (iii) furnish false or fraudulent material information in a record or report required by the act;[125] or (iv) present false or fraudulent identification when receiving a listed chemical,[126] are subject to criminal fines, imprisonment, or both.[127] Additionally, registrants who violate the aforementioned provisions may be subject to injunctive or declarative actions filed by the Attorney General in federal district court.[128]

Finally, the CSA specifies several offenses regarding listed chemicals. For example, criminal fines and/or imprisonment are available for any person who knowingly or intentionally (i) possesses a listed chemical with the intent to manufacture a controlled substance without proper registration; (ii) possesses or distributes a listed chemical with knowledge or a reasonable belief that the listed chemical will be used to manufacture a controlled substance; or (iii) evades the CSA's recordkeeping and reporting requirements by receiving or distributing listed chemicals in small units.[129] Also, any person who knowingly possesses or distributes listed chemicals in violation of the CSA, or knowingly violates the CSA's recordkeeping requirements, is subject to criminal fines, imprisonment, or both.[130] Furthermore, in addition to the other applicable penalties, violators of the aforementioned provisions may also be enjoined for up to ten years from handling listed chemicals.[131]

EXCEPTIONS TO THE REGULATORY REQUIREMENTS UNDER THE CSA

It is important to note that the CSA allows for exceptions and also exempts certain individuals from some or all of its regulatory requirements. For example, individuals exempted from registration requirements include, among others, officers or employees of the DEA, officers of the U.S. Customs Service, offers or employees of the U.S. Food and Drug Administration, and any other federal officers who are authorized to possess, import, or export controlled substances in the course of their official duties.[132] Officers or employees of any state, or political subdivision of a state, who are engaged in enforcement of state or local laws relating to controlled substances, are also exempt from registering with the DEA.[133] A person who has lawfully obtained, and who possesses, a controlled substance for his own use is also not required to register.[134]

In addition, only those actually engaged in activities relating to manufacturing, distributing, and dispensing controlled substances are required to obtain registration, but related or affiliated persons who are not engaged in such activities are not required to register. For example, a stockholder or parent corporation of a corporation that manufactures controlled substances is not required to obtain registration, nor are employees of a registered manufacturer, distributor, or dispenser.[135]

The DEA Administrator may, by regulation, waive the registration requirement for certain manufacturers, distributors, or dispensers, if he finds it consistent with the public health and safety.[136]

In certain circumstances, the CSA recordkeeping provisions do not apply. The CSA recordkeeping provisions do not apply to the prescribing or administering of a controlled substance in Schedules II-V by practitioners acting in the lawful course of their professional practice *unless* such substance is prescribed or administered in the course of maintenance or detoxification treatment of an individual.[137] For example, the prescribing or administering of methadone for the treatment of narcotic addiction must be in conformity with the CSA's recordkeeping provisions. The CSA also does not apply to research conducted in conformity with the exemption granted under certain provisions of the Federal Food, Drug, and Cosmetic Act (FFDCA) or to preclinical research or teaching.[138]

APPENDIX. CLASSIFICATION OF CONTROLLED SUBSTANCES

Schedule	CSA Statutory Provision	Examples of Scheduled Substances
Schedule I	Pursuant to 21 U.S.C. § 812(b)(1), a substance will be placed in Schedule I based on specific findings made by the Administrator that "(A) The drug or other substance has a high potential for abuse. (B) The drug or other substance has no currently accepted medical use in treatment in the United States. (C) There is a lack of accepted safety for use of the drug or other substance under medical supervision."	Heroin, lysergic acid diethylamide (LSD), marijuana, MDMA (Ecstacy), methaqualone (Quaalude), synthetic marijuana.[a]
Schedule II	Pursuant to 21 U.S.C. § 812(b)(2), a substance will be placed in Schedule II based on specific findings made by the Administrator that "(A) The drug or substance has a high potential for abuse. (B) The drug or other substance has a currently accepted medical use in treatment in the United States or a currently accepted medical use with severe restrictions. (C) Abuse of the drug or other substance may lead to severe psychological or physical dependence."	Methadone, methamphetamine, methylphenidate (Ritalin®), morphine, oxycodone (OxyContin®), phencylidine (PCP).[b]
Schedule III	Pursuant to 21 U.S.C. § 812(b)(3), a substance will be placed in Schedule III based on specific findings made by the Administrator that "(A) The drug or other substance has a potential for abuse less than the drugs or other substances in schedules I and II. (B) The drug or other substance has a currently accepted medical use in treatment in the United States. (C) Abuse of the drug may lead to moderate or low physical dependence or high psychological dependence."	Anabolic steroids, synthetic delta—9 tetrahydrocannabinol (THC), codeine, hydrocodone with aspirin or Tylenol®.[c]
Schedule IV	Pursuant to 21 U.S.C. § 812(b)(4), a substance will be placed in Schedule IV based on specific findings made by the Administrator that "(A) The drug or other substance has a low potential for abuse relative to the drugs or other substances in schedule III. (B) The drug or other substance has a currently accepted medical use in treatment in the United States. (C) Abuse of the drug or other substance may lead to limited physical dependence or psychological dependence relative to the drugs or other substances in schedule III."	Xanax®, Valium®, Equanil®, Talwin®, Darvon®.[d]

(Continued)

Schedule	CSA Statutory Provision	Examples of Scheduled Substances
Schedule V	Pursuant to 21 U.S.C. § 812(b)(5), a substance will be placed in Schedule V based on specific findings made by the Administrator that "(A) The drug or other substance has a low potential for abuse relative to the drugs or other substances in schedule IV. (B) The drug or other substance has a currently accepted medical use in treatment in the United States. (C) Abuse of the drug or other substance may lead to limited physical dependence or psychological dependence relative to the drugs or other substances in schedule IV."	Certain cough medicines with codeine, and certain opium preparations.[e]

a. *See* 21 C.F.R. § 1308.11(b)-(f) (complete listing of Schedule I drugs and substances); *see also* 21 C.F.R. § 1308.11(g) (temporary listing of substances subject to emergency scheduling in Schedule I).

b. *See* 21 C.F.R. § 1308.12(b)-(g) (complete listing of Schedule II drugs and substances).

c. *See* 21 C.F.R. § 1308.13(b)-(g) (complete listing of Schedule III drugs and substances).

d. *See* 21 C.F.R. § 1308.14(b)-(f) (complete listing of Schedule IV drugs and substances).

e. *See* 21 C.F.R. § 1308.15(b)-(e) (complete listing of Schedule V drugs and substances).

End Notes

[1] 21 U.S.C. §§ 801 et seq.

[2] *See* 21 C.F.R. § 1304.11(a) ("Each inventory shall contain a complete and accurate record of all controlled substances on hand ..."); *see also* 21 C.F.R. § 1301.74(a) ("All applicants and registrants shall provide effective controls to guard against theft and diversion of controlled substances ...").

[3] For a detailed summary of the CSA's criminal provisions, *see* CRS Report RL30722, *Drug Offenses: Maximum Fines and Terms of Imprisonment for Violation of the Federal Controlled Substances Act and Related Laws*, by Brian T. Yeh.

[4] This report does not cover all the requirements under the CSA, nor does it address state controlled substances regulations. Although federal and state governments both regulate controlled substances, federal law preempts state law when state law conflicts with the CSA. 21 U.S.C. § 903.

[5] 21 U.S.C. §§ 811-812.

[6] For the purposes of the CSA, the term "control" as defined by 21 U.S.C. § 802(5) means "to add a drug or other substance, or immediate precursor, to a schedule under [§ 812 of the act], whether by transfer from another schedule or otherwise."

[7] The procedures for these actions are found at 21 U.S.C § 811.

[8] 21 U.S.C. § 811(a).

[9] Although the CSA grants to the Attorney General the authority to enforce its provisions, 21 U.S.C. §§ 801 et seq., the Attorney General has delegated this authority to the DEA Administrator at 28 C.F.R. § 0.100(b). Accordingly, the term "Administrator" will be used instead of the term "Attorney General" for the remainder of this report.

[10] 21 U.S.C. § 811(b).

[11] The medical and scientific evaluations are binding on the DEA with respect to such matters and form a part of the scheduling decision. The recommendation on the initial scheduling of a substance is binding only to the extent that if HHS recommends that the drug or substance not be controlled, the DEA may not add it to its schedules. *Id.*

[12] *Id.*

[13] *See* 21 U.S.C. § 811(c)(1)-(8) (complete listing of factors Administrator must consider when determining control or removal of substances from schedules).

[14] *See* 21 U.S.C. § 812(b) ("[A] drug or other substance may not be placed in any schedule unless the findings required for such schedule are made with respect to such drug or other substance"). For a summary of the findings necessary for Schedules I-V, *see* **Appendix**.

[15] P.L. 98-473.

[16] 21 U.S.C. § 811(h)(1).

[17] *Id.*

[18] 21 U.S.C. § 811(4).

[19] 21 U.S.C. § 811(h)(3).

[20] 21 U.S.C. § 811(h)(2), as amended by the Synthetic Drug Abuse Prevention Act of 2012, P.L. 112-144.

[21] P.L. 100-690.

[22] Domestic Chemical Diversion Control Act of 1993, P.L. 103-200; Comprehensive Methamphetamine Control Act of 1996, P.L. 104-237; Methamphetamine Anti-Proliferation Act of 2000, P.L. 106-310; Combat Methamphetamine Epidemic Act of 2005, P.L. 109-177.

[23] The 40 listed chemicals are set forth at 21 C.F.R. § 1310.02(a) and (b).

[24] *See* 21 U.S.C. §§ 802(33)—(35) and 21 C.F.R. §§ 1300.02(b)(17)—(19) (defining listed chemicals).

[25] 21 C.F.R. § 1300.02(b)(18) defines the term "List I chemical" as "a chemical specifically designated by the Administrator in [21 C.F.R.] § 1310.02(a) ... that, in addition to legitimate uses, is used in manufacturing a controlled substance in violation of the [CSA] and is important to the manufacture of a controlled substance."

[26] 21 C.F.R. § 1300.02(b)(19) defines the term "List II chemical" as "a chemical, other than a List I chemical, specifically designated by the Administrator in [21 C.F.R.] § 1310.02(b) ... that, in addition to legitimate uses, is used in manufacturing a controlled substance in violation of the [CSA]."

[27] 21 C.F.R. § 1300.02(b)(18).

[28] 21 U.S.C. §§ 802(32)(A) and (B).

[29] *See* 21 U.S.C. § 813 ("A controlled substance analogue shall, to the extent intended for human consumption, be treated, for the purposes of any Federal law as a controlled substance in schedule I").

[30] United Nations Office on Drugs and Crime, *Synthetic Drugs*, *at* http://www.apaic.org/index.php?option=com_content&view=article&id=91&Itemid=63.

[31] *Drug Enforcement Administration, Schedules of Controlled Substances: Temporary Placement of Three Synthetic Cathinones Into Schedule I*, 76 Fed. Reg. 65371 (Oct. 21, 2011).

[32] For more information on this law and this topic generally, *see* CRS Report R42066, *Synthetic Drugs: Overview and Issues for Congress*, by Kristin M. Finklea and Lisa N. Sacco.

[33] The procedures for these scheduling actions are found at 21 U.S.C. § 811(d).

[34] Drug Enforcement Administration, *Electronic Prescriptions for Controlled Substances,* 75 Fed. Reg. 16235, 16237 (Mar. 31, 2010).

[35] According to 21 C.F.R. § 1300.02(b)(24), the term "registrant" means "any person who is registered [with the DEA] pursuant to [21 U.S.C. §§ 823 or 957]."

[36] DEA, *Disposal of Controlled Substances by Persons Not Registered With the Drug Enforcement Administration,* 74 Fed. Reg. 3480, 3481 (January 21, 2009).

[37] DEA, *Definition and Registration of Reverse Distributors*, 70 Fed. Reg. 22591 (May 2, 2005).

[38] 21 U.S.C. § 822; 21 C.F.R. Part 1301.

[39] 21 C.F.R. §§ 1301.22-1301.24 (exempting agents of registrants, certain military personnel, and law enforcement officials from DEA registration requirements).

[40] 21 U.S.C. § 802(27).

[41] 21 U.S.C. § 822(c)(3).

[42] DEA, *Definition and Registration of Reverse Distributors*, 68 Fed. Reg. 41222, 41226 (proposed July 11, 2003).

[43] 21 C.F.R. § 822(a).

[44] 21 C.F.R. § 1301.13.

[45] *Id.*

[46] 21 U.S.C. § 821; *see also* 21 C.F.R. § 1301.13(e)(1) (chart detailing specific types of registrations and respective fees).

[47] 21 U.S.C. § 822(f); 21 C.F.R. § 1301.31.

[48] 21 U.S.C. § 823.

[49] 21 U.S.C. §§ 823(a)-(f).

[50] 21 U.S.C. § 824(a) states in pertinent part: "A registration pursuant to section 823 of this title to manufacture, distribute, or dispense a controlled substance or a list I chemical may be suspended or revoked by the [Administrator] upon a finding that the registrant—

(1) has materially falsified any application filed pursuant to or required by this subchapter or subchapter II of this chapter;

(2) has been convicted of a felony under this subchapter or subchapter II of this chapter or any other law of the United States, or of any State, relating to any substance defined in this subchapter as a controlled substance or a list I chemical;

(3) has had his State license or registration suspended, revoked, or denied by competent State authority and is no longer authorized by State law to engage in the manufacturing, distribution, or dispensing of controlled substances or list I chemicals or has had the suspension, revocation, or denial recommended by competent State authority;

(4) has committed such acts as would render his registration under section 823 of this title inconsistent with the public interest as determined under such section; or

(5) has been excluded (or directed to be excluded) from participation in a program pursuant to section 1320a—7(a) of [the Social Security Act, which excludes certain individuals and entities from participation in Medicare and State healthcare programs] . . ."

[51] 21 U.S.C. § 824(c).

[52] 21 U.S.C. § 824(d); 21 C.F.R. § 1301.36(e).

[53] THOMAS C. FOX, CAROL COLBORN LOEPERE & JOSEPH W. METRO, HEALTH CARE FINANCIAL TRANSACTIONS MANUAL § 20:62 (2005).

[54] 21 C.F.R. § 1301.52.

[55] 21 C.F.R. § 1301.52(b).

[56] 21 C.F.R. § 1301.12.

[57] *See* United States v. Clinical Leasing Service, Inc., 925 F.2d 120 (5th Cir. 1991).

[58] Section 3(b) of P.L. 110-425, amending 21 U.S.C. § 823(f).

[59] 21 U.S.C. § 827; 21 C.F.R. Part 1304.

[60] 21 U.S.C. § 827(a)(3); 21 C.F.R. § 1304.21(a).

[61] 21 U.S.C. § 827(b)(3); 21 C.F.R. § 1304.04(a).

[62] *Id.*

[63] 21 U.S.C. § 842(a)(5).

[64] 21 U.S.C. § 843(a)(4).

[65] *See generally* 21 C.F.R. Part 1310 (records and reports of listed chemicals).

[66] 21 U.S.C. § 830(a) and (b); 21 C.F.R. §§ 1310.03-06.

[67] *See* chart at 21 C.F.R. § 1310.12(c).

[68] For the purposes of the CSA, the term "distribute," as defined by 21 U.S.C. § 802(11), means "to deliver (other than by administering or dispensing [to an ultimate user or research subject]) a controlled substance or listed chemical."

[69] 21 C.F.R. Part 1305.

[70] DEA Form 222 is only issued to customers who are properly registered with the DEA.

[71] 21 C.F.R. § 1305.13(c).

[72] 21 C.F.R. § 1305.13(d).

[73] 21 C.F.R. § 1305 Subpart C.

[74] 21 C.F.R. § 1305.29.

[75] 21 C.F.R. §§ 1304.31 and 1304.32.

[76] 21 C.F.R. § 1304.33.

[77] 21 C.F.R. § 1304.33(d).

[78] Section 3(c) of the Ryan Haight Online Pharmacy Consumer Protection Act of 2008, P.L. 110-425, adding new 21 U.S.C. § 827(d)(2). However, pharmacies are exempt from such reporting requirement if they do not exceed in a given month either of two thresholds: (1) 100 or more prescriptions dispensed, or (2) 5,000 or more dosage units of all controlled substances combined. *Id.*

[79] An "online pharmacy" means a person, entity, or Internet site, whether in the United States or abroad, that knowingly or intentionally delivers, distributes, or dispenses, or offers or attempts to deliver, distribute, or dispense, a controlled substance by means of the Internet, but does *not* include, among other things, (1) manufacturers and distributors who do not dispense controlled substances to an unregistered individual or entity, (2) advertisements that do not attempt to facilitate an actual transaction involving a controlled substance, or (3) a registered pharmacy whose dispensing of controlled substances via the Internet consists solely of refilling or filling new prescriptions for controlled substances in schedule III, IV, or V. 21 U.S.C. § 802(52), as added by section 3(a) of P.L. 110-425.

[80] Section 3(d) of P.L. 110-425, adding new § 311 to the Controlled Substances Act.

[81] *Id.*

[82] According to 21 U.S.C. § 802(10), the term "dispense" means "to deliver a controlled substance to an ultimate user or research subject by, or pursuant to the lawful order of, a practitioner, including the prescribing and administering of a controlled substance and the packaging, labeling or compounding necessary to prepare the substance for such delivery."

[83] According to 21 U.S.C. § 802(21), the term "practitioner" means "a physician, dentist, veterinarian, scientific investigator, pharmacy, hospital, or other person licensed, registered, or otherwise permitted, by the United States or the jurisdiction in which he practices or does research, to distribute, dispense, conduct research with respect to, administer, or use in teaching or chemical analysis, a controlled substance in the course of professional practice or research."

[84] *See* 21 C.F.R. § 1306.03 (persons entitled to issue prescriptions).

[85] 21 C.F.R. § 1306.04; United States v. Moore, 4223 U.S. 122 (1975).

[86] Pharmacists share with practitioners the responsibility to ensure that controlled substances are properly prescribed and dispensed. Both practitioners and pharmacists are subject to the criminal and civil provisions of the CSA for knowingly prescribing and dispensing a controlled substance in a manner inconsistent with the act. 21 C.F.R. § 1306.04(a).

[87] 21 U.S.C. § 829(a); *see also* 21 C.F.R. § 1306.05 (manner of issuance of prescriptions for Schedule II controlled substances).

[88] 21 U.S.C. § 829(a); *see also* 21 C.F.R. § 1306.11(b) (authorizing individual practitioners to administer or dispense controlled substances directly to patients without prescription).

[89] 21 C.F.R. § 290.10.

[90] 21 C.F.R. § 1306.11(d).

[91] 21 C.F.R. § 1306.05.

[92] 21 U.S.C. § 829(b). If the prescription is made orally, the pharmacist must promptly reduce to writing all of the information required to be in a prescription under 21 C.F.R. § 1306.05, except for the signature of the practitioner. 21 C.F.R. § 1306.21(a).

[93] 21 U.S.C. § 829(b); 21 C.F.R. § 1306.21(b).

[94] Drug Enforcement Administration, *Electronic Prescriptions for Controlled Substances,* 75 Fed. Reg. 16235, 16307 (Mar. 31, 2010).

[95] *See* 21 C.F.R. § 1306.13(a) ("The partial filling of a prescription for a substance listed in Schedule II is permissible if the pharmacist is unable to supply the full quantity called for in a written or emergency oral prescription.... The remaining portion of the prescription may be filled within 72 hours of the first partial filling").

[96] 21 U.S.C. § 829(a)("No prescription for a controlled substance in schedule II may be refilled.").

[97] 21 U.S.C. 829(b); 21 C.F.R. § 1306.22(a).

[98] Drug Enforcement Administration, *Electronic Prescriptions for Controlled Substances,* 75 Fed. Reg. 16235, 16316 (Mar. 31, 2010).

[99] Section 2 of the Ryan Haight Online Pharmacy Consumer Protection Act of 2008, P.L. 110-425, adding new 21 U.S.C. § 829(e).

[100] *Id.*

[101] *See* 21 U.S.C. §§ 826(a)-(e) (general provisions regarding the establishment of production quotas for Schedule I and II controlled substances).

[102] 21 C.F.R. §§ 1303.11(b)(1)-(5).

[103] *See* 21 C.F.R. § 1301.71 (general security requirements and standards for measuring compliance).

[104] 21 C.F.R. § 1301.71(b) states: "Substantial compliance with the standards set forth in §§ 1301.72-1301.76 may be deemed sufficient by the Administrator after evaluation of the overall security system and needs of the applicant or registrant." Section 1301.71(b) also sets forth a list of fifteen discretionary factors for Administrator to consider when evaluating the overall security system of an applicant or registrant; *see also* 21 C.F.R. § 1309.71(a)-(c) (general security requirements for List I chemicals).

[105] 21 C.F.R. § 1301.71(c).

[106] *See* 21 C.F.R. §§ 1301.72(a)(1)(i)-(iii) (specifications required for safes and steel cabinets storing Schedule I and II drugs or substances); *see also* 21 C.F.R. §§ 1301.72(a)(2) and 1301.72(a)(3)(i)-(vi) (specifications required for vaults storing Schedule I and II drugs or substances).

[107] *See* 21 C.F.R. § 1301.75 (physical security controls for practitioners).

[108] 21 C.F.R. § 1301.76(b).

[109] 21 C.F.R. § 1301.76(a).

[110] 21 C.F.R. § 1301.90.

[111] For information about disposal by patients who possess already dispensed controlled substances (as opposed to DEA registrants that want to dispose of them), *see* CRS Report R40548, *Legal Issues Relating to the Disposal of Dispensed Controlled Substances*, by Brian T. Yeh. This report discusses the Secure and Responsible Drug Disposal Act of 2010, P.L. 111-273, which, among other things, amended the Controlled Substances Act to allow a patient to deliver controlled substances to an entity that is authorized by federal law to dispose of them, providing that such disposal occurs in accordance with regulations issued by the Attorney General to prevent diversion of controlled substances.

[112] DEA, *Definition and Registration of Reverse Distributors*, 70 Fed. Reg. 22591, 22592 (May 2, 2005).

[113] Under 21 C.F.R. § 1307.21, any person may request permission from DEA to dispose of controlled substances without the need for a DEA or state government witness. If a registrant has a regular need to dispose of controlled substances, the DEA may grant blanket

authorization for such disposal; however, "DEA normally requires that the registrant provide two designated responsible individuals to accompany the drugs to the disposal site and witness the destruction." DEA, *Definition and Registration of Reverse Distributors*, 70 Fed. Reg. 22591 (May 2, 2005).

[114] A "reverse distributor" is a DEA-registered entity "who receives controlled substances acquired from another DEA registrant for the purpose of—(1) returning unwanted, unusable, or outdated controlled substances to the manufacturer or the manufacturer's agent; or (2) where necessary, processing such substances or arranging for processing such substances for disposal." 21 C.F.R. § 1300.01(b)(41).

[115] For a description of the criminal penalty provisions of the CSA, *see* CRS Report RL30722, *Drug Offenses: Maximum Fines and Terms of Imprisonment for Violation of the Federal Controlled Substances Act and Related Laws*, by Brian T. Yeh.

[116] 21 U.S.C. §§ 841(c); (e)-(f).

[117] 21 U.S.C. § 842.

[118] 21 U.S.C. § 843.

[119] 21 U.S.C. § 842(a)(2).

[120] 21 U.S.C. § 842(a)(5).

[121] 21 U.S.C. § 842(a)(6).

[122] *See generally* 21 U.S.C. § 842(c) (penalties for committing prohibited acts set forth in § 842(a)).

[123] 21 U.S.C. § 843(a)(1).

[124] 21 U.S.C. § 843(a)(2).

[125] 21 U.S.C. § 843(a)(4)(A).

[126] 21 U.S.C. § 843(a)(4)(B).

[127] *See generally* 21 U.S.C. § 843(d) (penalties for committing prohibited acts set forth in § 843(a)).

[128] 21 U.S.C. § 843(f).

[129] 21 U.S.C. §§ 841(c)(1)-(3).

[130] *See* 21 U.S.C. § 841(f)(1) and (2) (penalties for offenses involving listed chemicals).

[131] 21 U.S.C. § 841(e).

[132] 21 C.F.R. § 1301.24(a)(1).

[133] 21 C.F.R. § 1301.24(a)(2). For additional registration exceptions, see 21 C.F.R. §§ 1301.22-1301.23.

[134] 21 U.S.C. § 822(c).

[135] 21 C.F.R. § 1301.11(a); 21 U.S.C. § 822(c).

[136] 21 U.S.C. § 822(d).

[137] 21 U.S.C. §§ 827(c)(1)(A), 827(c)(1)(B).

[138] 21 U.S.C. § 827(c)(2).

INDEX

D

E

F

G

H

I

J

L

M

N

O

P

U

V

W

Y